OBSESSIVE COMPULSIVE DISORDERS: CHALLENGES AND SOLUTIONS

A MANUAL FOR TREATING PROFESSIONALS

---OCD---Tourette's Disorder---Trichotillomania---Hypochondriasis---Body Dysmorphic Disorder--- Aspergers Syndrome---Impulse Control Disorders (Compulsive Hoarding, Compulsive Shopping)

WITH

DR. CHRISTIAN R. KOMOR
OCD RECOVERY CENTER OF AMERICA

Obsessive-Compulsive Disorders: A Comprehensive Program for Recovery

BY THE END OF THIS MANUAL YOU WILL....

- Be able to effectively diagnose and differentiate between all of the eight major Obsessive-Compulsive Spectrum Disorders.

- Know the current brain research, genetics, and biological basis for these neurological conditions.

- Utilize a *Sixteen Keys To Recovery* plan for creating optimal relief for your obsessive-compulsive clients.

- Know how to effectively conduct various types of exposure and response-prevention based behavioral therapy.

- Recognize the four reasons why behavior treatment of obsessive-compulsive disorders often fails and how to avoid these pitfalls.

- Be equipped with a Seven-Step plan for supporting clients through difficult OCD moments and exposure and response prevention behavior therapy.

- Deal effectively with clients who suffer from "Pure-Obsessions".

- Know research-based Integrative Healthcare options for augmenting psychoactive medications and behavior therapy.

- Learn dozens of tools for providing your clients with anxiety reduction and self-care

- Pass the *optional open book exam* for Certification by The OCD Recovery Center of America

- Be able to build (or expand) a flourishing practice in a critical specialty area.

Today well lived, makes every yesterday
a dream of happiness and every
tomorrow a vision of hope.
- Sanskrit Proverb

FOR MORE INFORMATION ABOUT OBSESSIVE COMPULSIVE DISORDERS CONTACT:

The OCD Recovery Center
P.O. Box 6654
Grand Rapids, Michigan 49516
www.ocdrecoverycenter.com

WELCOME

Welcome. This publication is designed to provide a broad overview of the diagnosis, treatment practices, and procedures used in assisting individuals in achieving substantial recovery from obsessive-compulsive spectrum (OC Spectrum) disorders. Because this information is intended for both lay and professional audiences, it has been written in a style that combines technical information with practical advice. This style has the benefit of reaching a broader audience, but the drawback that it may at times seem cumbersome or disjointed. It is hoped the reader will appreciate the content and be accepting of any stylistic oddities. As we have learned time and again at the OCD Recovery Center, "nothing works for everyone all the time".

No creation exists in a vacuum. While many of the concepts presented in this manual are original and unique to the OCD Recovery Center program, various sections of the text find their origins in the outstanding work of friends and colleagues including: Thomas F. Crum (Key Fourteen); Jon Kabat-Zinn; James Callner; Edward Bourne, Lorraine Armitage and Joanne Kolean (Key Six); Steven Phillipson; Michael Jenike; Jeffery Schwartz; John March; Bruce Hyman, Andrew Weil (Key Five) and Thomas Komor.

Obsessive-Compulsive Disorder (OCD) and its associated "OC spectrum" disorders are chronic neurobehavioral problems with genetic origins and learned behavioral components. While medication and cognitive-behavioral psychotherapy generally have a significant impact on OCD, even under optimal conditions these interventions provide a maximum of only 60% of OC sufferers with 60% relief. Due to the chronic nature of OCD, recovery often comes slowly and with a good deal of struggle and energy utilization. Crises and setbacks are common and frequent. Also, exposure-base behavioral therapy and pharmaceutical interventions do not address the myriad complex lifestyle issues, which are part and parcel of the obsessive-compulsive experience. True recovery from OCD and its sister disorders requires a comprehensive approach drawing from a variety of disciplines and technologies.

Medication and exposure and response prevention (ERP) behavioral therapy often serve as the centerpieces in the recovery process. But for the majority of persons with OCD, it is essential to develop lifestyle behaviors that will augment medication and ERP. Eventually these approaches will a revitalized life based on serenity, spontaneity, and self-ownership. A person with OCD often thinks and approaches life differently as well. These differences can create ongoing loss of spontaneity, subclinical depression, life stress, conflict in relationships and blocks to spiritual and personal growth. Technologies for living must be learned so that every part of life contains the seed of progressive forward motion. It is these *comprehensive* recovery components that make the OCD Recovery Center approach to treatment unique.

Please note that the concepts and strategies presented in this paper, while applying most closely to the needs of OC sufferers with OCD also have wide applicability to related OC disorders including Hypochondriasis, Body Dysmorphic Disorder, Trichotillomania and Tourette's Syndrome.

As mentioned above, Obsessive-Compulsive (OC) Spectrum Disorders are, for the most part, genetically determined neurological disabilities. Due to their chronic nature they can be compared accurately to disabling diseases such as Diabetes or Parkinson's Disease. Few individuals report complete and total recovery from the disorder. More often OC sufferers report that their condition has improved to the point where it is still present, but not very bothersome or does not interfere unduly with their daily life.

Unlike sufferers of many other chronic neurological diseases, OC sufferers experience symptoms that are primarily *internal* and difficult to observe from the outside. Because of this the sufferer often feels isolated and misunderstood. OCD receives relatively little attention from the media, public agencies, and healthcare organizations. Efforts are now underway to increase awareness among OC patients of the rights open to them through the American with Disabilities Act.

People with OC disorders are also likely to try and hide their symptoms. With most of the suffering experienced and expressed internally, the OC sufferer is able to prevent others from becoming aware of the effects. This secrecy, of course, hampers treatment efforts and makes it even more difficult for the OC sufferer to make the critical shift in awareness to seeing the problem as a brain disorder rather than a personal failing.

THE OBSESSIVE-COMPULSIVE SPECTRUM DISORDERS

Our first task in understanding and treating obsessive-compulsive disorders is to learn which disorders are typically included in the spectrum and why. Let us first address the question of why.

The (Infamous) Cortical-Striatal-Thalamic Pathway

At the present time the best evidence available from various brain-imaging research points to the Cortical-Thalamic-Striatal pathway as being the site of dysfunction in obsessive-compulsive disorders.

An understanding of the organization of segregated, parallel, corticostriatal circuits has evolved over the past decade. The essential feature of note appears to be that there are several parallel, segregated circuits which share a fundamental organization. Projections from specific portions of the cortex converge in sub-territories of the striatum, which then send efferent's fibers through other basal ganglia structures to influence activity within particular thalamic nuclei. These circuits are then closed via projections from the thalamus back to the original territories within the prefrontal cortex.

Because there also are reciprocal projections from the cortex to the thalamus, bypassing these corticostriatal collaterals, the thalamic targets are positioned to serve a gating function both for thalamocortical and corticothalamic output. The balanced interrelationship of the direct and indirect pathways within the corticostriatothalamic collateral provides a mechanism for titrating the net influence of the striatum on the thalamus. This arrangement likewise provides a substrate for diseases that reflect disruption of this fine balance.

These segregated, parallel, corticostriatothalamic collateral pathways each sub serves a different class of functions corresponding to the topography of the cortex, striatum, and thalamus involved. The circuits have been categorized according to various schemes, which primarily differ regarding their level of complexity, including: sensorimotor, oculomotor, dorsal cognitive, ventral cognitive and affective-motivational corticostriatal circuits.

The sensorimotor circuit projects from primary and associated sensorimotor cortex via the putamen, to the ventral tier nuclei of the thalamus, and plays some role in sensorimotor functions. The oculomotor circuit projects primarily from frontal eye fields via the body of the caudate nucleus to the ventral anterior and medial dorsal nuclei of the thalamus. It plays a role in eye movements. The dorsal cognitive circuit projects from primarily dorsal, anterior, and lateral regions of prefrontal cortex via the dorsolateral portion of the head of the caudate nucleus, to the ventral anterior and medial dorsal nuclei of the thalamus. This circuit plays a role in complex cognitive processes including working memory and the ability to establish and shift mental sets.

The ventral cognitive circuit projects from anterior and lateral orbitofrontal cortex via the ventromedial portion of the caudate nucleus, also to the ventral anterior and medial dorsal nuclei of the thalamus, and plays a role in cognitive processes, such as response inhibition, especially related to social or emotional subject matter. The affective-motivational circuit projects from paralimbic cortical territories (i.e., posteromedial orbitofrontal cortex and the anterior cingulate) via nucleus accumbens (i.e., ventral striatum) to the medial dorsal nucleus within the thalamus, and plays a role in emotional or reward-based information processing. This circuit also is influenced heavily by enervation from limbic structures per se, such as the amygdala.

Through this oversimplified model, the striatum is presented as functionally homogeneous. The chart below outlines in simplified form the...

ELEMENTS OF SEGREGATED PARALLEL CORTICOSTRIATOTHALAMIC CIRCUITS

Structural Elements

Circuits	Cortex	Striatum	Thalamus
Sensorimotor	Sensorimotor	Putamen	Ventral tier nuclei
Oculomotor	Frontal eye fields	Caudate (body)	Medial dorsal and Anterior nuclei
Dorsal cognitive	Lateral prefrontal	Caudate (dorsolateral)	Medial dorsal and Anterior nuclei
Ventral cognitive	Anterior and lateral Orbitofrontal	Caudate (ventromedial)	Medial dorsal and Anterior nuclei
Affective/motiv.	Paralimbic	Nucleus accumbens	Medial dorsal nucleus

THE OC SPECTRUM OF DISORDERS

Below one will find a listing of the disorders the OCD Recovery Center believes are, or should be included in the OC Spectrum. They are listed under the category in which they are placed in the Diagnostic and Statistical Manual of Mental Disorders IV and also in order according to the frequency with which they are encountered at the OCDRC. A brief description of our conceptualization of each is included. Following this one will find a reproduction of the DSM-IV description and diagnostic criteria. Please note that the emphasis in this manual will be on the Anxiety, Impulse Control, and Somatoform disorders because of the frequency and depth of our experience with them.

Anxiety Disorders

Obsessive-Compulsive Disorders
- OCD
- Hoarding
- Symmetry
- Repeating
- Compulsive Slowness
- "Pure Obsessing"
- Checking
- Counting

Impulse Control Disorders

Trichotillomania

Somatoform Disorders

Hypochondriasis

Body Dysmorphic Disorder

Disorders First Diagnosed in Childhood

Tourette's Disorder

Stereotypic Movement Disorders

Aspergers Syndrome

THE SIXTEEN KEYS TO RECOVERY

At the *OCD Recovery Centers of America* we have developed sixteen basic "Keys To Recovery" that we have found helpful to our OC sufferers. Using these Sixteen Keys, we will provide an outline of the many tools now available for OC spectrum recovery including those falling within the realm of complementary and integrative medicine.

- ❖ **First Key: Accurate & Complete Diagnosis**

- ❖ **Second Key: Information, Education & Understanding Including OC Cycles**

- ❖ **Third Key: Assessing History & Damage from Disorder & Grieving Losses**

- ❖ **Fourth Key: Understanding Core Family of Origin Patterns and Psychological Dynamics**

- ❖ **Fifth Key: Identifying & Transcending Core Fears**

- ❖ **Sixth Key: Identifying & Finding Alternatives for Unhelpful Self-Medicators**

- ❖ **Seventh Key: Initiating and Refining Psychoactive &, or Phytomedicinal Medication Support**

- ❖ **Eighth Key: Initializing Specialized Complementary & Integrative Healthcare (CIH) Tools**

- ❖ **Ninth Key: Learning Stress & Anxiety Management Techniques**

- ❖ **Tenth Key: Developing Lifestyle Management & Self-Care Skills**

- ❖ **Eleventh Key: Developing Cognitive Restructuring & Obsession Inoculation Strategies**

- ❖ **Twelfth Key: Conducting Behavioral Therapy**

- ❖ **Thirteenth Key: Strengthening Family & Peer Relationships**

- ❖ **Fourteenth Key: Re-establishing a Healthy Doing-Being Balance**

- ❖ **Fifteenth Key: Repairing or Rebuilding Career & other Life Infrastructure Areas**

- ❖ **Sixteenth Key: Developing Relapse Prevention Plan Including Emergency Plan & Ongoing Resource/Support Utilization**

Some of the specific elements normally included in the Five Stage recovery process are:

- ✓ Establishing or confirming diagnoses.
- ✓ Identifying specific obsessions and compulsions.
- ✓ Identifying related problem areas such as depression or social anxiety.
- ✓ Identifying co morbid OC spectrum disorders.
- ✓ Establishing a current objective measure of symptom severity.
- ✓ Education, information, and didactic learning.
- ✓ Understanding the neurobiological and genetic nature of OC disorders
- ✓ Learning to externalize the disorder.
- ✓ Accepting the chronic nature of the disease.
- ✓ Stabilizing pharmacological, phytomedicinal and related supports.
- ✓ Developing lifestyle management and self-care skills:
- ✓ Anxiety reduction and management.
- ✓ Self-care, affirmation, and life enjoyment.
- ✓ Obsession inoculation training.
- ✓ Cognitive restructuring.
- ✓ Support resources.
- ✓ Social relationships and peer support.
- ✓ Spiritual self-care.
- ✓ Cognitive Behavioral Therapy (CBT)
- ✓ Establishing Patterns for Ongoing Exposure and Response (ERP) Prevention Work.
- ✓ Setting ongoing ERP and CBT goals.
- ✓ Aftercare Planning:
- ✓ Avoiding old OCD patterns.
- ✓ Integrating continuing self-care...

THE OCD CYCLE

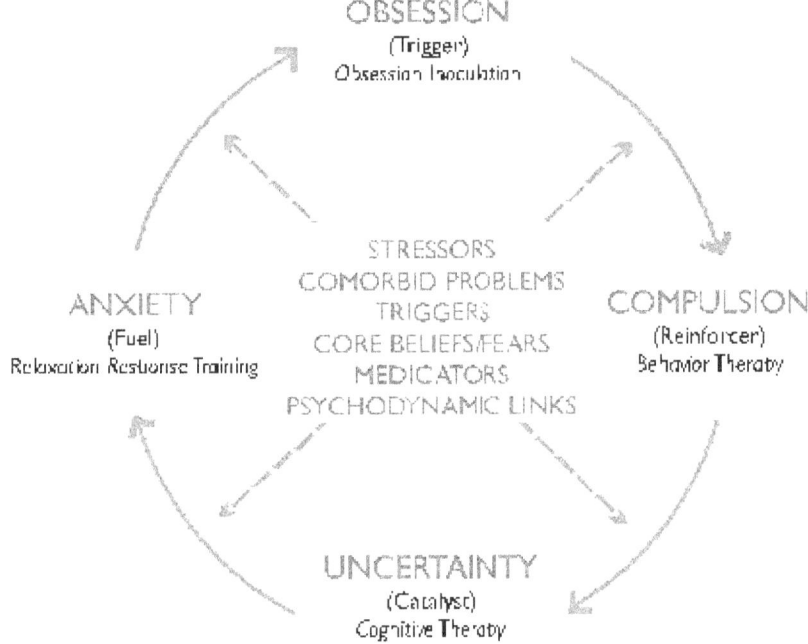

OBSESSION
(Trigger)
Obsession Inoculation

COMPULSION
(Reinforcer)
Behavior Therapy

ANXIETY
(Fuel)
Relaxation Response Training

STRESSORS
COMORBID PROBLEMS
TRIGGERS
CORE BELIEFS/FEARS
MEDICATORS
PSYCHODYNAMIC LINKS

UNCERTAINTY
(Catalyst)
Cognitive Therapy

NOTE   Comorbid problems may include: Depression, Phobias,
Seasonal Depression, Post-Traumatic Stress Disorder,
ADD/ADHD, or other OC Disorders.

THE FIVE STAGES OF OCD RECOVERY

Each person with an OC spectrum disorder is unique. It is amazing in fact, how many different permutations and nuances OC disorders can find to express themselves. Nevertheless, when we examine the recovery process itself, there appear to be five general stages in the recovery journey:

Stage I: The individual knows that something is wrong, but is not sure quite what it is. He or she has not received, or has not accepted the diagnosis of OC spectrum disorder. In this stage obsessions seem real and believable and the individual feels that the only way to neutralize them and be safe is to do what the voice of OCD is asking.

Stage II: The sufferer receives a diagnosis of OC disorder and begins to identify its' characteristics. An understanding of the neurological underpinnings of the disorder is arrived at. One begins to mobilize resources for treating it, including professional help and educational resources. The ability to refuse to perform compulsions begins in this stage. Grieving for losses related to the disorder and honestly appraising the effects it has had on our career, intimate relationships, etc. starts.

Stage III: Exposure and response prevention behavioral therapy begins in earnest. The individual takes a more structured approach to refusing rituals and confronting anxiety. A new lifestyle, self-care patterns, and mastery of complementary and alternative healthcare skills begin.

Stage IV: Habituation has now taken place to a significant degree and the individual has made changes to their brain function through the exposure and response prevention feedback cycle. They have also made inroads into working through family of origin issues related to the OC disorder and have identified and are transforming *core* anxiety-generating fears.

Stage V: Although he or she still experiences obsessions, the individual is able to distinguish them rapidly and to prevent them from having control over choices and actions. The individual spends significant amounts of time during the day experiencing freedom of choice and spontaneity. He or she has developed a strong support system and modified their lifestyle with the understanding that he or she is still prone to anxiety and obsession. Self-care and complementary healthcare procedures and practices are a solid part of the day. Joy and feelings of serenity, peace, and aliveness are experienced on a fairly regular basis. An appreciation for "just being" – enjoying the experience of being alive through the five senses is acquired and honed.

INITIAL MIND-BODY CONVERSATION

PRESENTING PROBLEM(S)
HISTORY OF PRESENTING PROBLEM(S)
CURRENT STRESSORS AND FEARS
HEALTH CARE STATUS
ENERGY
MENTAL STATUS
TENDENCY TOWARD ILLNESS
SLEEP
MEDICATIONS
SUPPLEMENTS A.1'IlD VITAMINS
NUTRITION AND RELATIONSHIP WITH FOOD ALCOHOL, CAFFINE, TOBACCO, ETC.
CURRENT AND PRIOR HEAL THCARE INTERVENTION
MARITAL OR PRIMARY RELATIONSHIPS
CURRENT FAMILY EVIRONMENT AND CHILDREN, OCCUPATION AND PRIMARY ACTIVITIES
PERSONAL HISTORY
FAMILY OF ORIGIN
PARENTS
SIBLINGS
PIVOTAL LIFE EVENTS
EDUCATIONAL EXPERIEINCES
RESOURCES
REST AND RELAXA TION
SPIRITUALITY
JOYS AND FEARS
PERSONALITY TRAITS
MENTAL AND EMOTION STATUS
STRENGTHS AND WEAKNESSES
RELATIONSHIPS AND SOCIAL SUPPORT
DAILY SCHEDULE
COPING PRACTICES AND MEDICATORS
TRIGGERS
IMAGES OF HEALTH
PREFERRED LEARNING MODALITIES

PSYCHOPHYSIOLOGIC RULE/OUT AREAS FOR OC DISORDERS

(1) HYPOGLYCEMIA

(2) ALLEGIES AND IMMUNE RESPONSE

(3) MINERAL DEFICIENCIES

(4) EXCESS LIVER TOXICITY

(5) HEAVY METALS

(6) ADRENAL EXHAUSTION

(7) THYROID IMBALANCE

SPECIAL CHARACTERISTICS OF OC POPULATION

    i. Memory problems including:
  1. Memory confidence
  2. Incidental memory
  3. Memory for linguistic gist

   ii. Learning difficulties including:
  1. Set shifting
  2. Delayed alternation
  3. Temporal order
  4. Judging self-performance
  5. Response inhibition

  iii. Altered circadian rhythms

  iv. Early morning increase in symptoms

   v. Self-esteem issues and shame

  vi. Social impairment

 vii. Emotional discontrol (esp. anger) in more severe OC.

viii. Reassurance seeking

  ix. Present focused and myopic life view

ASSESSING OC SYMPTOMS

Obsessions

Ordering and Organizing Obsessions
(Examples)

o Preoccupation with exactness, or perfect order
o Having handwriting be perfect or "just so"
o Compiling information, files, papers, or other items a certain "perfect" way

Religious Obsessions, Scrupulosity
(Examples)

o Having blasphemous thoughts or saying bad things
o Concern about religious beliefs
o Extreme right and wrong, morality
o Preoccupation with religious images or thoughts

Somatic Obsessions
(Examples)

o Strong worries about illness
o Rumination over a particular part of the body
o Anxiety about negative reactions to one's appearance

Contamination Obsessions
(Examples)

o Environmental contaminants-radon, asbestos, radiation, toxic waste
o Touching animals
o Fear of insects
o Becoming ill by contamination
o Making others ill by contaminating them
o Diseases such as AIDS, hepatitis, sexually transmitted diseases
o Bodily waste, secretions, urine, feces, saliva, blood
o Dirt or germs
o Household cleansing agents or chemicals

Hoarding, Saving, and Collecting Obsessions
(Examples)

o Urge to know or remember certain things-slogans, license plate numbers, names, words, events of the past
o Picking up items from the ground
o Filling empty space
o Throwing things away, even seemingly useful items
o Collecting useless things

Aggressive Obsessions
(Examples)

o Causing harm to self
o Causing harm to others
o Possibility of acting on unwanted impulses (stab someone, hit someone, etc.)
o Imagined responsibility for a terrible accident ("Hit and run OCD")
o Fear of blurting out insults or obscenities
o Doing something embarrassing or looking foolish
o Violent or horrific images in the individual's mind causing one to do harm to others

Sexual Obsessions
(Examples)

o Being or becoming a homosexual
o Thoughts of sexual violence
o Sexualized thoughts, images, or impulses
o Thoughts about molesting the individual's own or other children

Timeline Contamination and Calendar Obsessions
(Examples)

o Magical idea that present can be contaminated by past
o Magical idea that the future can be contaminated by the present
o Magical idea that one's consciousness can be pulled into the past
o Continual need to review dates or excessive preoccupation with calendar

Perfectionistic Obsessions
(Examples)

o Fear of saying something wrong, not saying something just right, or leaving out details
o Worry about losing things
o Worry about making mistakes

Symmetry Obsessions
(Examples)

o Having items in environment lined up or ordered perfectly
o Preoccupation with color matching
o Making certain that events are scheduled or synchronized

Somatosensory Obsessions
(Examples)

o Upset by certain sounds and noises-clocks ticking, loud noises, buzzing
o Sensitive to the feel of clothing or textures on the skin
o Intrusive nonsense sounds, music, words
o Excessive focus on bodily functions, health, or physical appearance
o Unusual need to pick at seams or stroke certain surfaces

Superstitious Obsessions
(Examples)

o Fear of saying certain words because of obsessional beliefs
o Fear of using certain colors for superstitious reasons
o Fears about deviating from certain patterns of counting, walking around ladders, walking between oil spots on the pavement, etc.
o Concern with lucky and unlucky numbers.

Relationship Obsessions
(Examples)

o Inability to let go of needing to control another person's behavior
o Extreme over-protectiveness
o Stalking
o Sacrificing self-care to be around another person
o Fantasizing continually about a relationship

Compulsions

Reassurance-Seeking Compulsions
(Examples)

o Continual need to share thoughts, feelings, ideas, and reactions with others
o Marked difficulty in being alone for more than short periods
o Constant questioning of others about appropriateness of one's own behavior
o Excessive need to repetitively ask others for reassurance
o Need to confess wrong behavior, even the slightest insignificant infractions of behavior toward others

Cleaning and Washing Compulsions
(Examples)

o Excessive or lengthy hand washing
o Showering or bathing for excessive amounts of time, often in a ritualistic way
o Tooth brushing, grooming, shaving, etc. that is excessive or ritualistic
o Continual cleaning of things in one's environment
o Avoidance of any objects considered "contaminated" by "germs" or thoughts
o Avoidance of specific places-cities, towns, buildings-considered "contaminated"
o Concern with wearing gloves or other protection to avoid "contamination"

Hoarding, Saving, and Collecting Compulsions
(Examples)

o Saving, collecting seemingly useless items
o Need to pick up useless items from the ground
o Difficulty throwing things away

Gambling or Risk Taking Behavior Compulsions
(Examples)

o Inability to refuse dares made to self or by others
o Gambling for excessive lengths of time or beyond financial means
o Inability to stay away from dangerous activities (fireworks, car racing, etc.)
o Repeatedly engaging in risky sex
o Taking extreme risks which may compromise health status

Checking Compulsions
(Examples)

o Checking that one did not make a mistake
o Checking an aspect of physical condition such as blood pressure, or heart beat
o Checking that one did not harm others without realizing it
o Checking that one did not harm the OC sufferer with realizing it
o Checking safety of physical surroundings-locks, windows, appliances, stoves
o Checking that boxes, closets or jars are closed

Safety Compulsions
(Examples)

o Checking one did not do something that lead to future harm
o Taking excessive steps to prevent harm to self or others-for example,
   avoidance of certain objects or extreme precautions to prevent unlikely harm or danger

Mental Ritual Compulsions
(Examples)

o Mental rituals-prayers, repeating "good" thoughts to counteract "bad" thoughts
   performed with the intention of reducing or neutralizing anxiety.
o Superstitious behavior that takes excessive amounts of time
o Need to touch, tap, or rub certain items or people

Repeating, Counting, Ordering Compulsions
(Examples)
o Reading and rereading things, sometimes for hours
o Excessive worrying that one didn't understand something one read
o Excessive writing and rewriting things
o Repeating routine activities-going in and out of doorways, repeated crossing of
   thresholds, getting up and down from a chair, combing hair, tying shoes, dressing and
   undressing over and over
o Doing certain activities a particular number of times
o Counting items-books on a shelf, ceiling tiles, cars going by
o Counting during compulsive activities, such as checking and washing
o Arranging items in a certain order-books, pencils, cupboards

Food-Related Ritual Compulsions
(Examples)

o Eating ritualistically according to specific "rules"
o Arranging food or utensils in ritualistic manner
o Refusing to eat except at certain times or under certain conditions
o Eating foods in a particular order

Spending, Shopping or Acquiring Compulsions
(Examples)

o Compulsive shopping
o Hoarding purchased items
o Shopping for excessive lengths of time or in ritualistic patterns
o Buying a great number of items due to fear of running out

22

WEEKLY BEHAVIOR AND SYMPTOM CHANGE LOG

<u>SUNDAY</u>   WEEK OF: _____   NAME: _____   *KEY: 0 = None 100 = Highest Possible*

Today's Projects: _____

Anxiety AM	0--------------25---------------50----------------75--------------100	Comments: _____
Anxiety PM	0--------------25---------------50----------------75---------------100	_____
Depression AM	0--------------25---------------50----------------75---------------100	_____
Depression PM	0--------------25---------------50----------------75---------------100	_____
Obsessions AM	0--------------25---------------50----------------75---------------100	_____
Obsessions PM	0--------------25---------------50----------------75---------------100	_____
Compulsions AM	0--------------25---------------50----------------75---------------100	_____
Compulsions PM	0--------------25---------------50----------------75---------------100	_____
Other AM	0--------------25---------------50----------------75---------------100	_____
Other PM	0--------------25---------------50----------------75---------------100	_____

Today's Discoveries: _____

_____

MONDAY

Today's Projects: _____

Anxiety AM	0--------------25---------------50----------------75--------------100	Comments: _____
Anxiety PM	0--------------25---------------50----------------75---------------100	_____
Depression AM	0--------------25---------------50----------------75---------------100	_____
Depression PM	0--------------25---------------50----------------75---------------100	_____
Obsessions AM	0--------------25---------------50----------------75---------------100	_____
Obsessions PM	0--------------25---------------50----------------75---------------100	_____
Compulsions AM	0--------------25---------------50----------------75---------------100	_____
Compulsions PM	0--------------25---------------50----------------75---------------100	_____
Other AM	0--------------25---------------50----------------75---------------100	_____
Other PM	0--------------25---------------50----------------75---------------100	_____

Today's Discoveries: _____

_____

TUESDAY

Today's Projects: _____

Anxiety AM	0--------------25---------------50----------------75--------------100	Comments: _____
Anxiety PM	0--------------25---------------50----------------75---------------100	_____
Depression AM	0--------------25---------------50----------------75---------------100	_____
Depression PM	0--------------25---------------50----------------75---------------100	_____
Obsessions AM	0--------------25---------------50----------------75---------------100	_____
Obsessions PM	0--------------25---------------50----------------75---------------100	_____
Compulsions AM	0--------------25---------------50----------------75---------------100	_____
Compulsions PM	0--------------25---------------50----------------75---------------100	_____
Other AM	0--------------25---------------50----------------75---------------100	_____
Other PM	0--------------25---------------50----------------75---------------100	_____

Today's Discoveries: _____

_____

WEDNESDAY

Today's Projects: _____

Anxiety AM	0--------------25---------------50----------------75--------------100	Comments: _____
Anxiety PM	0--------------25---------------50----------------75---------------100	_____
Depression AM	0--------------25---------------50----------------75---------------100	_____
Depression PM	0--------------25---------------50----------------75---------------100	_____
Obsessions AM	0--------------25---------------50----------------75---------------100	_____
Obsessions PM	0--------------25---------------50----------------75---------------100	_____
Compulsions AM	0--------------25---------------50----------------75---------------100	_____
Compulsions PM	0--------------25---------------50----------------75---------------100	_____
Other AM	0--------------25---------------50----------------75---------------100	_____
Other PM	0--------------25---------------50----------------75---------------100	_____

THURSDAY

Today's Projects: _____

Anxiety AM	0---------------25---------------50---------------75--------------100	Comments: _____
Anxiety PM	0---------------25---------------50---------------75--------------100	_____
Depression AM	0---------------25---------------50---------------75--------------100	_____
Depression PM	0---------------25---------------50---------------75--------------100	_____
Obsessions AM	0---------------25---------------50---------------75--------------100	_____
Obsessions PM	0---------------25---------------50---------------75--------------100	_____
Compulsions AM	0---------------25---------------50---------------75--------------100	_____
Compulsions PM	0---------------25---------------50---------------75--------------100	_____
Other AM	0---------------25---------------50---------------75--------------100	_____
Other PM	0---------------25---------------50---------------75--------------100	_____

Today's Discoveries: _____

_____

FRIDAY

Today's Projects: _____

Anxiety AM	0---------------25---------------50---------------75--------------100	Comments: _____
Anxiety PM	0---------------25---------------50---------------75--------------100	_____
Depression AM	0---------------25---------------50---------------75--------------100	_____
Depression PM	0---------------25---------------50---------------75--------------100	_____
Obsessions AM	0---------------25---------------50---------------75--------------100	_____
Obsessions PM	0---------------25---------------50---------------75--------------100	_____
Compulsions AM	0---------------25---------------50---------------75--------------100	_____
Compulsions PM	0---------------25---------------50---------------75--------------100	_____
Other AM	0---------------25---------------50---------------75--------------100	_____
Other PM	0---------------25---------------50---------------75--------------100	_____

Today's Discoveries: _____

_____

SATURDAY

Today's Projects: _____

Anxiety AM	0---------------25---------------50---------------75--------------100	Comments: _____
Anxiety PM	0---------------25---------------50---------------75--------------100	_____
Depression AM	0---------------25---------------50---------------75--------------100	_____
Depression PM	0---------------25---------------50---------------75--------------100	_____
Obsessions AM	0---------------25---------------50---------------75--------------100	_____
Obsessions PM	0---------------25---------------50---------------75--------------100	_____
Compulsions AM	0---------------25---------------50---------------75--------------100	_____
Compulsions PM	0---------------25---------------50---------------75--------------100	_____
Other AM	0---------------25---------------50---------------75--------------100	_____
Other PM	0---------------25---------------50---------------75--------------100	_____

Today's Discoveries: _____

_____

INITIATING AND REFINING PSYCHOACTIVE AND, OR PHYTOMEDICINAL MEDICATION SUPPORT

- OC Disorders are direct manifestations of brain dysfunction; it is legitimate to look for treatment options among the various pharmaceutical resources available in psychiatric medicine.
- SRIs or SSRIs available by prescription. Prozac, Luvox, Zoloft, Paxil, and Celexa soon Lexapro are relatively effective in providing relief from obsessions, anxiety, and depression.
- About 40% of OC patients respond to medication and another 20% are "partial responders" but, recent meta-analysis suggests there is *only 20% improvement over placebo.*
- Expert Consensus - *Second Line treatment* (after behavioral interventions) in the treatment of OC disorders.
- Pharmacological management of OC spectrum disorders can be complex and protracted.
- It may take up to 16 weeks for an SRI medication to show an effect.
- Side effects are not insignificant. Seem to increase with severity, co morbidity and duration of disorder
- For tic and impulse control disorders: Risperidon, Zyprexa, Clozeril, Pimozide, Haldol. .
- Medications can also sometimes lose their effectiveness over time - up to 20% for depression, but much less for OC.
- Often depression will persist after the OCD remits with medication. Lithium and
- Wellbutrin often used in these situations.
- Relapse rate is over 90% when medication is stopped if no behavior therapy has accompanied the medication. (Relapse could be delayed up to 3 months.)
- Obsessions and compulsions seem to respond equally to medication.
- Data is scant on their long-term side effects. European data not encouraging.
- Next evolution in psychopharmacology will be the use of advanced brain scanning techniques, such as SPECT, PET, and FMRI scans, to pinpoint problem areas in the brain and target drugs to resolve those problems identified.
- Currently advisable that individuals who suspect they have an OC disorder to seek diagnosis from a psychiatric psychopharmacologist. Disorders are too complex to be treated by professionals who have not made a special study of them and kept up with current literature and emerging treatment innovations.
- The degree or type of *physical side effects* (gastritis, sexual dysfunction, headaches, etc.) or anxiety *about* taking a medication has no predictive value in terms of drug efficacy.
- An escalation of psychological symptoms (e.g. heightened anxiety, increased depression, increased obsessions, or compulsions) very often *is predictive* of drug efficacy. This information can be used to provide encouragement to patients suffering through the initial side effects of psychotropic medication for OC disorders.
- Patients often need encouragement - "Don't stop a minute before a miracle"
- Use the mental model of a cold or flu illness in order to view side-effects as uncomfortable - but only temporary.
- Start a medication during a time when stress and life changes are low.

- Advise patients to avoid focusing on side-effects mentally. Instead, log them down on a chart or journal and then go on to some pleasurable activity.
- Make sure to *increase* all available methods of self-care (e.g. taking hot baths, exercising, playing games, going to movies). It's OK to distract and sooth oneself in order to get through a temporary discomfort.
- For gastrointestinal effects take medication with food, stay on a bland diet for the time being (bananas, rice, apple sauce, dry toast = B.RA.T.), practice yoga, use a heating pad. Encourage patient to keep in mind thousands of people have been through this as well. For sleep problems obtain a copy of our Sleep Hygiene Protocol available at www.mindbodyconsult.com
- Subset of OC sufferers, for whom SSRI/SRI medications seem to lose effectiveness either partially or completely once administered, discontinued and then restarted. Advise patients to taper very slowly down once per week (or even less often for very long-acting medications) so that it can be determined what their individual response to the decrease will be. Far easier to increase the dose once more than to reinitiate the medication altogether.
- For individuals who are free of a personal family history of Bipolar Disorder, the over the counter drug SAi\1e (taken in doses from 400 to 1,200 milligrams AlVI apart from meals) often appears to speed up and enhance SSRI/SRI response.
- For patients with uncomplicated and fairly mild OC situations it may be possible for the patient to take a supplement (e.g. Acupuncture, St. John's Wort, Inositol, etc.) rather than or in addition to prescription medication. This should be done under close supervision of a Naturopathic Physician or other practitioner trained in the use of psychoactive phytomedicinals and procedures. The OCD Recovery Center specializes in this area and we frequently consult with other practitioners around the US.
- Combined treatment with several different agents may be necessary in resistant forms of OC disorders. This is also true where co-morbid depression, thought disorder, or high anxiety are present.

THERAPEUTIC STARTING DOSES FOR SRI MEDICATIONS IN OCD TREATMENT

PROZAC (Fluoxetine)	**80 mg**
PAXIL (Paroxetine)	**60 mg**
ZOLOFT (Sertraline)	**200 mg**
LUVOX (Fluvoxamine)	**300 mg**
CELEXA (Citalopram)	**60 mg**
LEXAPRO (Escitalopram)	**40 mg**

Refractory Obsessive-Compulsive Disorder: State-of-the-Art Treatment

Eric Hollander, M.D.; Dontella Marazziti, M.D.; Steven A. Ramussen, M.D.,Luigi Ravizza, M.D,; Chawkie Benkelfat, M.D.; Sanjaya Saxena, M.D.; Benjamin D. Greenberg, M.D., Ph.D.; Yehuda Sasson, M.D.; and Joseph Zohar, M.D.

J Clin Psychiatry 2002;63{suppl 6}:20-29

Characterization of Non-responders Preliminary Results from the International OCG Treatment Refractory Consortium

- The large number of nonresponsive patients is difficult to characterize because of ambiguities in diagnostic criteria, the possible existence of subtypes, and high rate co-morbidity in these patients.

- Lack of a clear definition for non-responder.

- The ultimate data collection goal is 450 records. Preliminary results of 274 patients are currently available.

- Some findings were unexpected and paradoxical: treatment responders had a higher rate of family history of tics and more co-morbid impulsive aggressive disorder. Some of the data were as expected: non-responders had more severe illness, poorer insight, and more co-morbid bipolar and eating disorders.

- Responders also had a higher incidence of sudden onset of illness and episodic course of illness.

- No significant differences were noted between responders and non-responders on age, gender, age at onset, length of illness, or prominent symptom subtypes.

- Changing state seemed to be most associated with changing biology, and that happened mostly and dramatically in the CBT group.

- Results suggest that patients who respond have improvement in serotonin synthesis in key brain regions.

Review of Treatment Options for Non-responders

(1) Behavioral Therapy

(2) SSRIs and Clomipramine
- A trial of clomipramine is recommended (and vice versa).
- In patients aged 40 years and older, clomipramine should be given after an adequate work-up that includes an electrocardiogram (ECG) and rules out ophthalmologic problems (e.g. closed glaucoma)
- High doses of clomipramine are needed.

(3) Augmentation Options
Augmentation is called for when there is partial or no response to the above-mentioned approaches.

Risperidone.

Pindolol
Double-blind , however it appears to give an extra "push" to partial responders rather than actually turning non-responders into responders.

Lithium
The only double-blind, placebo- controlled study failed to find significant statistical difference.

Buspirone
Reports of its efficacy are conflicting. Started with doses of 5mg t.i.d. and advanced as tolerated to a therapeutic dose 30 to 60 mg/day, usually given in 3 divided doses for a period of 6 weeks.

Clomipramine
A common practice in non-responders, although double-blind studies of the efficacy of this approach are lacking. May lead to a substantial increase in the level of tricyclics in the blood.

Fenfluramine
No longer available

Trazodone
A controlled study was terminated prematurely because the investigators had not noticed a response.

Tryptophan
L- Trypophan, the amino acid precursor of serotonin, has been reported to be effective in OCD. However, one should be careful with trypothan augmentation, due to the safety issue (association between tryptophan and eosinophilia myalgia syndrome). The recommended dose of trypothan is 2 to 10g/day.

Thyroid hormones
A controlled study did not confirm this agent's efficacy in OCD.

Olanzapine
An atypical antipsychotic with less likelihood of extrapyramidal side effects than typical neuroleptics or risperidone, has shown promise as an adjunctive treatment for SRI-refractory OCD in open trials.

Olanzapine for Schizophrenia Patients with Nonresponsive OCD
About 25% of patients with schizophrenia also have obsessive-compulsive (OC) symptoms. In patients with both schizophrenia and OCD, there is exacerbation of OC symptoms following treatment with clozapine, risperidone, and olanzapine has been reported.

Clozapine
On the basis of the hypersensitivity hypothesis of OCD, chronic treatment might have beneficial effects. However, a study in which clazapine monotherapy was administered to 20 treatment – resistant OCD patients for 10 weeks reported a lack of efficacy. However, in another open case report, clozapine reduced OC symptoms. Moreover, other open reports suggest that a combination of clozapine and an SSRI reduce OC symptoms in schizophrenia.

SAMe
Case reports suggest this brain methyl donor may speed the effectiveness of other drugs and is safe to use in all known augmentation situations. It may reduce depression within one to two weeks.

5-HTP
Immediate precursor to serotonin. Very rare reports of esophilia myalgia syndrome.

Intravenous clomipramine
Daily infusions of clomipramine for 14 days, the maximum dose being 325 mg, or pulse loading of 150 mg on day 1 and 200 mg on day 2 followed, after a 4-day delay, by oral clomipramine.

Monoamine oxidase inhibitors (MAOIs).
No evidence to support

Clonazepam
The benzodiazepine also has effects on the sertonergic system, thus providing a theoretical explanation for its role in OCD. However, negative results were reported in one controlled study.

Inositol
An improvement in OCD was reported in one double-blind study.

Hypericum
Several open label studies suggest effectiveness. Can be combined with 5-HTP and SAMe, but not with SSRI of MAOI drugs.

Clonidine
The range of associated side effects and the lack of controlled studies hinder its use for OCD patients.

Electroconvulsive therapy (ECT) is not compelling, reserved for the symptomatic treatment of severely depressed and suicidal OCD patients.

Transcranial magnetic stimulation (TMS) a few cases suggest a potential for use of the technique.

Anti-androgen therapy

Neurosurgery
The last resort is neurosurgery. Current operations include anterior cingulotomy, anterior capsulotomy, subcaudate tractotomy, and limbic leucotomy. These procedures are helpful in some patients and are relatively safe, about 40% to 60% of patients would be expected to receive total or partial benefit from neurosurgery.

Special Conditions
If the diagnosis is OCD and a tic disorder, small doses pimozide or haloperidol in addition to the sertonergic drug are associated with a higher therapeutic response
Augmentation Strategies for Non-responders

Gabapentin
The y-aminobutyric acid (GABA) modulator Gabapentin was reportedly beneficial as an augmenting agent in a small open study in OCD patients. In the study of gabapentin plus fluoxetine in OCD, OCD patients with a minimum YBOCS score of 16, despite at least 3 months of fluoxetine monotherapy, received added gabapentin for a total of 6 weeks, titrated to a maximum and stable daily dose of 3600 mg over the first 2 weeks, or placebo in a randomized, crossover design. Preliminary data analysis indicated no improvement in YBOCS scores at the end of the gabapentin arm compared with placebo treatment. Preliminary analysis also suggested no enhancement of inhibitory processing on pTMS after chronic gabapentin treatment in the subset of patients undergoing pTMS.

(5) SWITCHING STRATEGIES FOR NONRESPONDERS

Venlafaxine
Venlafaxine, an SNRI similar to clomipramine but lacking the anticholinergic, antihistaminic, and a-adrenergic blocking effects, has been studied in the treatment of OCD.[1963-65]
These results indicate that venlafaxine may be as efficacious as clomipramine in the acute treatment of OCD but with fewer side effects and confirm and extend previous reports. Results indicate that after 2 failed SSRI trials, clinicians should consider switching OCD patients to clomipramine or venlafaxine. Given the better tolerability of venlafaxine with respect to clomipramine and the initial reports of an anti obsessional property of this agent, a switch to venlafaxine appears to be a reasonable alternative.

Switching SSRIs: Citalopram and Fluvoxamine
In OCD patients who failed trials with other SSRIs, switching to another SSRI may elicit a good response. Shifting from one SSRI to another may be effective because, although all these drugs block the serotonin transporter, their receptor profiles are different, which may explain the specificity of response, since faster titration may prevent the onset of side effect.

(6) NOVEL APPROACHES

Oral Morphine
A placebo-controlled, double-blind study '68 of oral morphine for treatment-resistant OCD hypothesized that once weekly oral morphine would benefit patients with treatment resistant OCD. Three of the 8 patients had a $\geq 40\%$ decrease in YBOCS score, and 1 had a 29% decrease. The mean decrease in YBOCS score was $26.2\% \pm 14.5\%$. No patient's YBOCS score increased in the week after morphine administration. A single dose of oral morphine is well tolerated and can substantially ameliorate OCD symptoms in some patients during the week after the dose. This finding suggests that other neurotransmitter and peptide systems may play a role, perhaps through their effects on other neurotransmitter systems.

Sumatriptan and 5-HT 10 Receptor Agonists
After considering the effects of 5- HT receptor agonists with different binding profiles on the symptoms of OCD, it may be hypothesized that the 5-HTID receptor is implicated in the pathophysiology of OCD. The OCD symptoms of 5 sumatriptan subjects worsened as measured by the YBOCS.

Anterior Gamma Capsulotomy
Patients received bilateral single lesions in the anterior limb of the internal capsule or bilateral double lesions placed just ventral to the initial lesion in the coronal plane. The single lesion was ineffective and not associated with a placebo response. The double lesion resulted in clinical improvement in 38% to 50% of patients in the 2 studies. There were no decrements in cognitive performance or adverse personality changes observed. The issue of risks and benefits from a gamma knife approach versus deep brain stimulation should be addressed in future research.

INTEGRATIVE HEALTHCARE FOR OC RECOVERY - TOP PICKS

- Qigong exercises (Video - Dr. Jerry Alan Johnson's Healing Workout 800-743   5608)

- Breathing (Audio - Dr. Andrew Weil 800-333-9185)

- Meditation (Audio - Dr. Andrew Weil and Dr. Jon Kabat-Zinn 800-333-9185) or...

- Attention Training (A TT)

- Exposure & Response Prevention (ERP) behavior therapy

- Inositol or...

- 5-Hyrdoxy-L-Tryptophane or...

- Cranial Electrical Stimulation (CES)

- Avoidance of sugar, caffeine and (usually) nicotine

- Calcium and magnesium supplementation

- Prayer

- Stress reduction and awareness of triggers and sensitivities

- Reduction of reassurance seeking

- Eight hours of sleep nightly

- Journaling

- Social and support groups

Warnings: The phytomedicinal and Integrative Healthcare information provided in this Key section is intended for educational purposes and may not be construed as a medical prescription or as a substitute for the advice of the individual's physician. Do not use or advise the use of these products and procedures without first consulting a physician especially if one is pregnant or lactating. Be advised that some herbs and dietary supplements can cause severe allergic reactions in some individuals and may also have an adverse result in conjunction with other medications, or treatments. One should regularly consult a physician and or psychopharmacologist in matters regarding the health, and particularly in respect to symptoms and conditions which may require diagnosis or medical attention. Reevaluate use of any of these products after 6 months. Dr. Christian R. Komor, the OCD Recovery Center of America, P.C.and Mind/Body Consulting Services, disclaim any liability arising directly or indirectly from the use of the following or preceding information.

ANXIETY SYMPTOMS

I. Mild Stage:

Physiological Response
Muscle tone is right for vital body functions
Vital signs are stable
Pupils are dilated
Speech is easily understood
Senses are sharpened
More talkative or more quiet
Emotional Response
Minimal feeling of being threatened by others or by situation
May feel some irritability

Cognitive Response
Learning can occur
Increased motivation to learn
Able to solve problems and learn effectively
Can think rationally
Acuity of sensory input sharpened

II. Moderate Stage

Physiological Response
Increased body tension, jumpy
Perspiring of palms and underarms
Increased pulse and respirations
Fatigue and headaches
Increased rate of speech
Gastrointestinal sensations like tightness in throat, butterflies in stomach, nausea, diarrhea, heartburn, belching
Difficulty sleeping at night
Dry mouth
May not hear someone talking
Muscles tight

Emotional Response
Feelings of nervousness
Irritability—especially to noise
Lonely
Worried
Increased concern about what is going on

Cognitive Response
Selective inattention
Tunnel vision—fails to notice what is occurring outside the immediate area of focus
Learning can occur but ability to think clearly is diminished
Ruminating
Focus on one aspect of situation

III. Severe Stage

Physiological Response
Perspire profusely; beads of sweat
Urge to defecate or urinate
Breathing—shallow and rapid
Speech—fast, constant, loud, or high pitched
Gastrointestinal symptoms more severe: nausea, vomiting, diarrhea
Respiratory symptoms include feeling like can't breathe
Chest pain, rapid heartbeat, feel like having a heart attack or going to die
Headache
Automatic repetitious behaviors occur, i.e. wringing hands
Speech is puzzling and bewildering to listener
Deafness may occur

Emotional Response
Feeling wooden, strange, or unreal
Angry
Crying
Feeling powerless, insecure, low self-esteem, inadequate
Feel helpless

Cognitive Response
Can't perceive whole situation or experiences
Learning blocked by anxiety
Tendency to jump from one unconnected topic to another
Preoccupied
Distracted
Focus on scattered details

IV. Panic Stage

Physiological Response
Physical function may be paralyzed after extended time
Increase in all physical symptoms
Aimless running or shouting or unable to move or speak
Communication is unclear and may be impossible to understand

Delusions/hallucinations

<u>Emotional Response</u>
Feelings of dread, terror, unreality
Feelings of dying
Eeriness

<u>Cognitive Response</u>
Severe stress; perceived detail is elaborated and blown up
Learning and information processed blocked
Poor reality testing
Unable to cooperate

V. Terror Stage

<u>Physiological Stage</u>
Immobilized, shakes
Life is threatened if not reduced quickly

Neurophysiology of Anxiety

Although it is the body's most important organ, the brain is totally dependent on circulating blood for its energy and is unable to store nutrients needed for continuous operation. Any stress on the brain decreases blood flow. Persons with panic disorder tend to show a decrease in brain blood flow when under even minimal stress. This in turn affects the amygdala, the para-hippocampal gyrus, hippocampus, the posterior hypothalamus, and the periaquiductal gray area of the brain all of which have been closely associated with anxiety disorders.

When then brain receives sensory input that suggests a situation being encountered may be threatened, a sequence of responses is initiated in the nervous system starting with the sensory nerve centers of the brain in the cerebral cortex (two bands called the sensory band and the motor band). Information about the perceived threat then travels to the…

Thalamus—(motor board of the individual's computer) takes on the information only

Amygdala—(seek or scan button) attaches fear; it is the fight or flight center, but has to consult the hippocampus before it knows whether or not to attach fear to it

Hippocampus—the librarian; "pulls all of the books off the shelf" to organize memory and pull it together

Pre-frontal Cortex—"Yes, But Committee"; re-assess, cause and effect-to not act on impulses

Parietal Lobe—Executive Secretary—gets everything packaged together, organized to send it to

Frontal Lobe—Board of Directors—cognition, thinking; decided thought or action; if action—goes to the motor board and we have a motor response

ANXIETY REDUCTION, LIFESTYLE MANAGEMENT AND INTEGRATIVE HEALTHCARE FOR OC DISORDERS

Relaxation Response – The Ultimate Goal

The term "relaxation response" was coined by cardiologist Herbert Benson in the late 1960's to describe the intentional triggering of the parasympathetic nervous system through various procedures. Most of the self-care and anxiety reduction procedures outlined below have in common the use of the relaxation response. Eliciting the relaxation response results in decreased metabolism, slowing of heart rate and respiration, decreased muscle tension and distinctive brain wave changes – all of benefit to people with high levels of anxiety and obsessive ideation. The relaxation response is being taught by Dr. Benson and his colleagues at Harvard University. (*Jacobs GD, and Lubar JF. Spectral analysis of the central nervous system effects of the relaxation response elicited by autogenic training.* Behavioral Medicine. *1989;15:125-32.*)

Acupressure
1. An ancient art using finger pressure on specific points to unblock, balance, or increase the circulation of life force energy in the body.
2. Research has shown that acupressure can be effective for treatment symptoms of stress.
3. Can be done on oneself or with another person.
4. The points can be used whenever symptoms occur or as a daily preventive practice.
5. With traumatic stress, energy is blocked or frozen in the tissues and muscles.
6. Tension in the muscles usually indicates a blockage of energy that has accumulated around an acupressure point.
7. Holding the acupressure point, the tension releases, permitting the energy to flow freely,—allowing the body to heal and balance itself naturally.

Acupuncture
Used in oriental and other cultures for hundreds of years, acupuncture and electroacupuncture have been more recently studied under controlled conditions by western medicine. Anesthesia, irritable bowel, headache, addiction, immune disorders, asthma and allergies, nausea, stroke and neurological impairment have all received attention in the acupuncture research literature. (*Edzard E, White R. Acupuncture for back pain: a meta-analysis of randomized controlled trials.* Archives of Internal Medicine. *1998;158:2235-2214.*)

Affirmations
Relaxing puts one in a suggestible state. Listening to a specially created tape is an ideal way to remind the OC sufferer of important affirmations, coping strategies, and new attitudes that one is striving to remember. The affirmations and reminders may change daily. Affirmations can involve specific relaxation instructions, suggestions for behavioral change, imagery for healing, suggestions for improved self-esteem, reminders to change something and assertions that everything will be okay.
- Make the affirmation positive
- Specific description of what one wants to achieve

- Works best if combined with an image, a mental picture of the change one wants to achieve.

Examples of helpful affirmations:
- "Each day I become more and more relaxed."
- "I accept my body feeling, every sensation."
- "I can relax away my stress."
- "I breathe deeply and calmly when I feel stress."
- "I am responsible for making myself feel good."
- "I can feel good."
- "I am kind and good."
- "I can stop the negative thoughts."

Aromatherapy

The use of specific aromatic scents to affect the psychological and physical condition of the body has been a part of many cultures throughout history. Genuine natural oils are diffused into the air resulting in possible effects on the immune, nervous, and other systems of the patient. Empirical literature is limited in this area of complementary healthcare but studies are increasingly available. For example, a recent study at Sloan -Kettering Hospital in New York found a 63% decrease in anxiety during medical procedures when subjects were exposed to oil of vanilla. *The Lancet* reported a study in which elderly patients were able to discontinue use of sleeping medication when exposed to oil of lavender at bedtime. Postpartum discomfort, colds, erectile dysfunction, and arthritis are some of the conditions which aromatherapy may have utility in alleviation of symptoms. (*Hay I, Jamieson M, Ormerod A. Randomized trial of aromatherapy: successful treatment for alopecia areata.* Archives of Dermatology. *1998;134:1349-1352.*)

Assertiveness Training

1. Teaches how to stand up for the individual's legitimate rights without bullying others or letting them bully others.
2. Assertiveness is the ability to express personal rights and feelings.
3. Goal is to increase the number and variety of situations in which assertive behavior is possible, and to decrease passivity or hostile blow ups.
4. Developing awareness and expression of the individual's thoughts, the individual's feelings, the individual's wants and needs.

Biofeedback /EEG Neurofeedback

Biofeedback ranges from heat-sensitive "stress dots" worn on the hand to measure thermal response of sympathetic and parasympathetic body changes to advanced multimodal electroencephalogram neurofeedback which can be used to retrain dysfunctional neural brain pathways. The research literature for the efficacy of biofeedback is extensive for a variety of medical and psychological problems. (*Tansey MA. A neurobiological treatment for migraine: the response of four cases of migraine to EEG biofeedback training.* Headache Quarterly. *1991;1:90-96.*)

1. Biofeedback is the use of instruments to detect and amplify specific physical states in the body that one usually doesn't notice, and to help bring them under voluntary control.

2. Gives immediate information about biological conditions such as muscle tension, temperature, brain wave activity, sweating blood pressure and heart rate.
3. Used to supplement other relaxation exercises.
4. Goal is to learn to lower muscle tension or blood pressure whenever one encounters a stressful situation.
5. Identify early signs of arousal and correct them before one becomes really stressed.
6. Very expensive
7. Requires training
8. In home machines

Bodywork

The term "bodywork" describes a group of procedures including various types of massage (Swedish, deep tissue, sports), connective-tissue work such as Rolfing, myofacial and craniosacral therapy and functional-educational approaches such as Feldenkrais, Trager Method, and the Alexander Technique. Of these, massage therapy is probably the best known and understood. Studies are underway to evaluate the use of these practices in medical settings such as Saint Mary's Hospital in Grand Rapids. (*Astin J, et al. A review of the incorporation of complementary and alternative medicine by mainstream physicians.* Archives of Internal Medicine. *1998;159:2303-2310.*)

Breathwork

1. Many different types of breathing exercises
2. Positive results for relaxation, hyperventilation and prelude to other interventions
3. Hyperventilation intervention—breathe slowly into cupped hands or into a paper bag. Mild hyperventilation remedy is simple—breathe through nose rather than mouth.
- Excellent audio tape available from Andrew Weil, M.D. 800-333-9185

Brief Muscle Relaxation

1. Close the eyes and sit quietly, letting go of any distracting thoughts (20 seconds)
2. Bend the arms, then cross them in front of the chest. Tighten the fists, arms, shoulders, chest and back, and lift the shoulders to the ears, while breathing (10 seconds). Now relax (15-20 seconds).
3. Crunch up the face, wrinkle the nose, squint the eyes, purse the lips, and bite down on the teeth (10 seconds).
4. Take a deep breath, pull in the stomach, and tense the lower back. Hold the breath while counting to six. Then exhale SLOWLY. Now relax (15-20 seconds).
5. Extend the legs and tense them, while pointing the toes toward the head (10 seconds). Now relax (15-20 seconds).
6. Repeat Steps 2-5.
7. Sit quietly, clearing the mind and focusing on gentle breathing or on a pleasant scene in the mind as one invites the body to feel relaxed, warm, and heavy (60 seconds).
8. Open the eyes, feeling refreshed and at ease.

Calming Breath

1. Place a hand on the chest and one on the abdomen. Take a deep breath in through the nose – feeling the breath deep in the throat – all the way down into the stomach so that the hand on the stomach rises while the hand on the chest remains in its original position. Count four with one inhale – hold for a count of four.
2. *Slowly* exhale to a count of 7, saying "relax" (or a similar word) under the breath.
3. Let the muscles go limp and warm; loosen the face and jaw muscles.
4. Remain in this "resting position" physically and mentally for a few seconds, or for a couple of natural breaths.

Calming Counts

1. Sit comfortably.
2. Take a long, deep breath and exhale it slowly while saying the work "relax" under the breath.
3. Close the eyes.
4. Take ten natural, easy breaths. Count down with each exhale, starting with "ten".
5. This time, while one is breathing comfortably, notice any tensions, perhaps in the jaw or forehead or stomach. Imagine those tensions loosening.
6. After reaching "one", open the eyes again.

Centering

Centering is a true mind/body technique developed initially for use in martial arts settings, especially in the arts of Aikido and Judo. Martial artists, ballet dancers and other athletes learn to maintain a *proactive* focus on the geographic center of their physical body – known in Japan as the "hara". In the case of the martial artist, centering facilitates maintenance of concentration on one's own movements rather than being distracted or drawn off into *reacting* to an opponent's behavior.

In daily life centering is often used in communications-skills training where people have become un-centered and are acting in an overly aggressive/forceful fashion or, (conversely) in an overly passive/submissive manner. Both imbalances tend to create interpersonal anxiety. A more "centered" response is to look inside and then make an "I statement" concerning ones thoughts or feelings. For example, "When you step on my foot I feel uncomfortable and I would like you to get off my foot" versus "You are a clumsy fool."

In anxiety disorders the mind/body act of centering can quickly shift the obsessive focus off of the person, object, or situation and back onto the reality of one's moment-by-moment experience. When we teach our OC sufferers to "center" we begin by asking them to focus their attention on the exact geographic middle of the physical body. That is a point an inch or two below the naval and in the center of the abdomen. Just as one can hold out the individual's hand in front of one and feel the sensation of opening and closing the fingers, one can develop a "feel" for this center point in the body.

Once a sense of this center point of physical anatomy is developed, it can be used as an intervention in times of high anxiety when obsessional cognitions have begun to take over. By focusing on this center point, attention shifts inward and internal balance becomes re-established.

In order to "test" one's centered state, simply ask someone to give a gentle push on the front of the individual's shoulder while standing side by side. The individual's immediate tendency will be to become aware of the touch on the shoulder. This is a metaphor for the way in which obsessions distract us from our center. When this occurs do not resist the touch on the shoulder (obsession) - this will only get one more caught up in it. Instead, just refocus the individual's attention on the center point - regarding the shoulder touch (obsession) as irrelevant to the individual's true needs, purpose, and goals. (Note: In the test situation, if one finds the individual's body wobbling when one is touched, it is likely that one is not centered. If one feels a sense of solidness and stability, one has mastered the centered state.)

Cognitive Behavioral Therapy

The thoughts, attitudes, and perspective we have about life as we live it play a big part in determining whether we suffer from anxiety and depression or experience energy and joy.

	Event Situation	Negative Cog	Cog. Distortion	Core Belief	Positive Cog.	Positive Action
1						
2						
3						
4						
5						
6						
7						

DEFINITIONS OF COGNITIVE DISTORTIONS

1. ALL-OR-NOTHING THINKING: One sees things in black-and-white categories. If the individual's performance falls short of perfect, one sees the OC sufferer as a total failure. When a woman on a diet ate a spoonful of ice cream, she told herself, "I've blown my diet completely." This thought upset her so much that she gobbled down an entire quart of ice cream.

2. OVERGENERALIZATION: One sees a single negative event, such as a romantic rejection or a career reversal, as a never-ending pattern of defeat by using words such as "always" or "never" when one thinks about it. A depressed salesman became terribly

upset when he noticed bird dung on the windshield of his car. He told himself, "Just my luck! Birds are *always* crapping on my car!"

3. MENTAL FILTER: One picks out a single negative detail and dwells on it exclusively so that the vision of reality becomes darkened, like the drop of ink that discolors the entire beaker of water. Example: One receives many positive comments about a presentation to a group of associates at work, but one of them says something mildly critical. Person obsesses about this for days and ignores all the positive feedback.

4. DISQUALIFYING THE POSITIVE: One rejects the positive experiences by insisting they "don't count" for some reason or other. In this way one can maintain a negative belief that is contradicted by the individual's everyday experiences. If one does a good job, one may tell own self that it wasn't good enough or that anyone could have done it as well. Discounting the positive takes the joy out of life and makes one feel inadequate and un-rewarded.

5. JUMPING TO CONCLUSIONS: One makes a negative interpretation even though there are no definite facts that convincingly support the individual's conclusion.
    a. MIND READING: One arbitrarily concludes that someone is reacting negatively and doesn't bother to check this out.
    b. THE FORTUNE TELLER ERROR: One anticipates that things will turn out badly, and feels convinced that the individual's prediction is an already-established fact. Before a test one may say, "I'm really going to blow it. What if I flunk?" If the person is depressed the fear may be, "I'll never get better."

6. MAGNIFICATION (CATASTROPHIZING) OR MINIMIZATIION: One exaggerates the importance of things (such as the individual's goof-up or someone else's achievement), or one inappropriately shrinks things until they appear tiny (the individual's own desirable qualities or the other fellow's imperfections). This is also called the "binocular trick."

7. EMOTIONAL REASONING: One assumes that the individual's negative emotions necessarily reflect the way things really are: "I feel it, therefore it must be true." Examples: "I feel terrified about going on an airplane. It must be dangerous to fly." Or "I feel guilty. I must be a rotten person." Or "I feel angry. This proves I am being treated unfairly." Or "I feel so inferior. This means I am a second-rate person." Or "I feel hopeless. It must really be hopeless."

8. SHOULD STATEMENTS: One tries to motivate the OC self with shoulds and shouldn'ts, as if one had to be whipped and punished before one could be expected to do anything. Thinks that things *should* be the way one hoped or expected them to be. After playing a difficult piece on the piano, a gifted pianist told herself, "I shouldn't have made so many mistakes." This made her feel so disgusted that she quit practicing for several days. "Musts" and "oughts" are also offenders. The emotional consequence is guilt. When one directs statements toward others, one feels anger, frustration, and resentment.

9. LABELING AND MISLABELING: This is an extreme form of overgeneralization. Instead of describing the individual's error, one attaches a negative label to the OC sufferer: "I'm a loser." When someone else's behavior rubs one the wrong way, one attaches a negative label to him: "He's a terrible louse." Mislabeling involves describing an event with language that is highly colored and emotionally loaded.

10. PERSONALIZATION AND BLAME: One sees the self as the cause of some negative external event, which in fact one was not primarily responsible for.

a. Personalization occurs when person holds self responsible for an event that isn't entirely in the individual's control. When a woman received a note that her child was having difficulties in school, she told herself, "This shows what a bad mother I am," instead of trying to pinpoint the problem so that she could help her child. When another woman's husband beat her, she told herself, "If only I were better in bed, he wouldn't beat me." Personalization leads to guilt, shame, and feelings of inadequacy.

b. Some people do the opposite. They blame other people for their problems, and they overlook ways they might be contributing to the problem: "The reason my marriage is so lousy is because my spouse is totally unreasonable." Blame usually doesn't work very well because other people will resent being scapegoated and they will just toss the blame right back in the individual's lap. It's like the game of hot potato—no one wants to get stuck with it.

1. All- or-nothing (dichotomous) thinking:
2. Arbitrary inference:
3. Disqualifying the Positive
4. Emotional Reasoning
5. Exaggerating/catastrophizing:
6. Jumping to Conclusions:
7. Labeling and Mislabeling:
8. Magnification (Catastrophizing) or Minimization:
9. Mental Filter:
10. Mind Reading:
11. Overgeneralization:
12. Personalization:
13. Should Statements:

Cranial Electrical Stimulation

Research on this innovation in electromedicine is limited at this time. This procedure has just recently been evaluated and approved by the Food and Drug Administration (FDA) for use in anxiety disorders and is being evaluated for use in clinical depression, headache, and insomnia. (*Klawansky et al. (1995). Meta-analysis of CES studies.* Journal of Nervous and Mental Disorders. *1995;183:478-485.*)
Available through Electromedical Products Corp. 800-367-7246

Dawn/Dusk Simulation

Studies in chronobiology have found that the human body operates on daily rhythmic cycles which affect in significant ways the function of many of our bodily systems. These "circadian" rhythms are in part determined by zeitgebers or "set points" such as meals, exercise, and sleep-wake patterns. Depression, sleep disorders, muscular disease, neurological and other psychophysiological disorders have been linked to disturbances in these circadian rhythms. Rapid illumination of one's sleeping quarters upon waking in the morning can bypass the brain's normal arousal process causing an important set point to be missed. Dawn simulation devices can be employed to gradually stimulate the reticular activating system of the brain inducing more normal waking zeitgeber function. (*Avery D, et al. Dawn simulation treatment of winter depression: a controlled study.* American Journal of Psychiatry. *1993;150:113-117.*)

Depression Treatment

As with anxiety, depression is such a common mind/body ailment that our office has developed a specific protocol to use for treatment. Various complementary procedures including Eye Movement Desensitization and Reprocessing (EMDR) are integrated with counseling tools such as psychodrama, relapse-prevention, assertiveness skills, and self-esteem to create a multimodal recovery plan. (*Ernst E, Rand J and Stevison C. Complementary therapies for depression.* Archives of General Psychiatry. *1998;55:1026-1032.*)

Electromagnetic Field Mitigation

While stationary direct current magnetic fields have been associated with positive effects on health, high milligause electromagnetic fields generated by electrical appliances, power lines and home wiring have been epidemiologically linked to cancer and brain tumors. Electromagnetic fields found in living environments can be measured and mitigated through various methods. (*Jackson JD. Are the stray 60-Hz electromagnetic fields associated with the distribution and use of electric power a significant cause of cancer?* Proceedings of The National Academy of Sciences. *1992;89:3508-3510.*)

EMDR—Eye Movement Desensitization Reprocessing

1. Research shows that it is rapid, safe and effective
2. Does not involve drugs or hypnosis. It is a simple, non-invasive OC sufferer-therapist collaboration.

3. Short-term therapy is effective for a wide range of disorders including chronic pain, phobias, depression, worry, recovery from sexual abuse and traumatic incidents.
4. Uses a natural function of the body-- rapid eye movement--as its basis.
5. The human mind uses REM during sleep time to help it process daily emotional experiences. When trauma is extreme, this process breaks down and REM sleep doesn't bring the usual relief.
6. Most effective when used in conjunction with other traditional methods of therapy.
7. Trained clinician only.
8. **USING EMDR IN OCD: A PROTOCOL**

   a. **Begin with imagery to activate obsession. (e.g. imagine hands are dirty)**
   b. **Set negative cognition (e.g. "I will catch a horrible disease and die."**
   c. **Set positive cognition. (e.g. "I'll be OK even if my hands are dirty.")**

      d. **Start hand movements using anxiety- provoking imagery + negative cognition**

      e. **Reduce SUDs to 25-75 level.**

      f. **Proceed to Invivo ERP.**

Engram Therapy

We are all continually imprinting, modeling and storing memories and associations as we go through our lives. Engrams are simply powerful associational pathways formed in our brain chemistry. For example, the smell of suntan lotion may trigger measurable psychological and physiological responses in our bodies similar to those we associate with a relaxing day at the beach. Attending deliberately to how we create and use these associational engrams can be a significant tool for healing and wellness.

Energy Therapy

There are various forms of energy therapy in practice today. These ancient techniques range from the belief in chi or ki energy in oriental medicine to the belief that God exerts an energetic force in corporal human affairs. Reiki is one form of "energy work" often encountered in the complementary healthcare field. Although research is ongoing, the empirical studies that have been conducted were unable to show a measurable energy effect beyond placebo. (*Rosa L, Rosa E, Sarner L, Barrett S. A close look at therapeutic touch.* Journal of the American Medical Association. *1998;279:1005-1010.*)

Environmental Medicine

The best healthcare practitioners have always looked beyond the symptoms of disease to the patient's environment. The roots of health and of dysfunction often lie in the individual's environment. Toxic substances, relationships, careers, and lifestyles can often be modified or replaced to reduce deleterious effects. (*Steinman D, Epstein S. The safe shopper's bible: a* consumer's guide to nontoxic household products, cosmetics and food. *New York, NY: Simon and Schuster Macmillan Company; 1995.*)

Exercise and Fitness Training

Exercise is one of the best documented of complementary healthcare practices. In vivo empirical studies have demonstrated clear cardiovascular, immune, respiratory, neurologic, gastrointestinal, and psychological health benefits from aerobic, flexibility and strengthening exercise. (*Leon AJ, Connett D. and Rauramaa R. Leisure-time physical activity levels and risk of coronary heart disease and death: the multiple risk factor intervention trial.* Journal of the American Medical Association. *1987;258:2388-95.*)

b. Any regular exercise routine is good.

c. People with anxiety should aim for aerobic conditioning.

d. Three to five days per week. Work up to 30-45 minutes a day. Short bursts, 10-15 minutes a day is great for decreasing stress. Some types of exercise are:

      i. `Walking

      ii. Swimming

      iii. Aerobics

      iv. Bicycling

      v. Dancing
     vi. Racquetball
    vii. Tennis
   viii. Kick boxing
     ix. Skating
      x. Skiing
     xi. Rowing
    xii. Rock climbing
   xiii. Running
   xiv. Basketball
    xv. Soccer

Friendly Self-Talk

a.) Onboard reminders such as slogans and fear fighting formulas
b.) Decreasing overvalued ideation
c.) Detaching from OCD "brain noise"
d.) Increasing self-esteem
e.) Feeling and expressing emotions
f.) Focus on the positive behaviors rather than the OCD.
g.) Providing self with rewards for any and all progress.
h.) Always de-escalate and relax
i.) Detaching and letting go
j.) Keeping focus on self
k.) Dis-inhibition and spontaneity
l.) Saying "No" to shoulds
m.) Choices and "wanting to"
n.) Saying "So what" and lightening up!
o.) Being self-responsible versus dependent
p.) Be kind to the OC sufferer – especially about the individual's OCD
q.) Living in the now
r.) Practicing acceptance
s.) Having appropriate expectations
t.) Fostering a "Just be - don't think" approach to living. OCD lives in the mind so it helps to redirect to experiences versus thoughts.
u.) Change the setting. Take a day off and go to the beach, grandparents, visiting friends, hiking, etc. Make note of positive changes experienced and take these experiential learning's back to the regular routine.
v.) Surrender to the feeling" (anxiety) instead of staying numb by doing the OCD.
w.) OCD co-varies with low self-esteem and not finding one's own voice. OCD is the final expression of self-denial - shoulds lead to OCD!
x.) If one does a ritual "behavior" at least follow it with an "exposure".

Guided Imagery

Researchers at George Washington University found that research subjects were able to rapidly learn mucosal immune imagery and direct the profusion of cytokines, differential T0Cells, and lymphocytes in their body. Treatment of depression, anxiety, chronic pain, immune and many other types of disorders all have been augmented significantly with the application of guided image therapy. Often audio tapes are employed to provide the patient with control over dose and frequency. (*Tusek D, et al. Guided imagery: a significant advance in the care of patients undergoing elective colorectal surgery.* Diseases of the Colon and Rectum. *1997;40:172-178.*)

1. Guided imagery or visualization can include:
    a. Receptive visualization—relax, empty the mind. Sketch a vague scene, ask a question, and wait for a response.
    b. Programmed visualization—create an image, include sight, taste, sound and smell. Imagine a goal one wants to attain or a healing that one want to accelerate.
    c. Guided visualization—visualize the scene in detail, but omit crucial elements. Then wait for the individual's subconscious or the inner guide to supply the missing pieces in the puzzle.

An Exercise
1. Get comfortable:
    Lie down or sit down
    Make sure that the back and neck are supported
2. Begin to relax:
    Focus on breathing
    Breathe slowly, deeply, and evenly until one begins to feel relaxed
3. Begin tensing and relaxing muscles:
    Tense right fist and arm for a few seconds, and then relax it
    Feel the difference between tensed and relaxed
    Again, tense right fist and arm for a few seconds and then relax
    Begin feeling in control of tension and relaxation
    Tense then relax left fist and arm in the same manner
    Feel the difference between tension and relaxation
    Again, tense left fist and are for a few seconds then relax
4. Proceed to tense and relax other muscle groups:
    Gently, tense then relax right leg (Repeat)
    Continue by gently tensing and relaxing left leg (Repeat)
5. Continue tensing and relaxing in the same manner as above:
    Eyes
    Jaw
    Shoulders
    Chest
    Stomach
    Hips
    Any other tense muscles (until completely relaxed)
6. Imagine a pleasant scene to enhance relaxation.
7. To strengthen visual imagery use other sensations such as feeling sun's warmth, a breeze on skin, fragrances, comforting sounds, tastes, etc.
8. Role-play interesting dialogue with someone in the scene to establish an interpersonal connection.
9. Complete relaxation by suggesting positive messages such as, "I feel relaxed," "It feels good to relax," "I feel in control," "I can relax, feel good, and feel in control whenever I want."
10. Repeat each day.

Heart Rate (Palpitation) Decreasing
1. Ice cold water drinking
2. Visualize slowing heart rate
3. Massage carotid artery (with MD okay)

Herbal Phytomedicinal Therapy
Herbs have always been an integral part of healthcare. Over 80% of the world's population uses phytomedicinal substances as their primary form of ingested healthcare. Although, as with synthetic drugs, 25-30% of patient response to phytomedicinal products is placebo-effect; herbs have the power to heal and, when used improperly, to kill. Essential, detailed information about the efficacy, safety and interactive effects of herbal preparations has been compiled by Mind/Body Consultant Services. We provide educational protocols for herbal, enzymatic, and hormonal use for disorders ranging from anxiety and depression to migraine headache and Attention Deficit Disorder. (*Miller L. Herbal medicinals: selected clinical considerations focusing on known or potential drug-herb interactions.* Archives of Internal Medicine. *1998;158:2200-2211.*)

Homeopathy
Homeopathy was founded by Samuel Christian Hahnemann (1755-1843) who developed the idea of "likes curing likes". Similar to the allopathic concept of inoculation, homeopathic medicine utilizes highly diluted substances to treat disease and psychological dysfunction. Practiced throughout much of the world and particularly in Europe, homeopathy has been criticized by allopathic medicine as being mainly a placebo. Recent studies, however, have shown that homeopathy is able to achieve statistically significant results under meta-analysis but not when considered for specific treatments for specific diseases. Further research is ongoing. (*Linde K, et al. Are the clinical effects of homeopathy placebo effect? A meta-analysis of placebo-controlled trails.* Lancet. *1997;350:834-43.*)

Humor Therapy
Humor is an important component of wellness and recovery. Humor allows us to achieve a health detachment for difficult life events. Humor also acts as a powerful social bond and assists with the development of relationships. Laughter has been associated with various health benefits including strengthened immune response and increased pain threshold. (*Cogan R, Cogan W, Waltz W and McCue. Effects of Laughter and relaxation on discomfort thresholds.* Journal of Behavioral Medicine. *1987;10:139-144.*)

Hydrotherapy
Thermal products such as water, mud and algae can be employed to treat a variety of psychological (e.g. anxiety, sympathetic nervous system hyperarousal) and physiological (e.g. psoriasis, muscle injury, stroke, headache) healthcare problems. Whirlpools, sitz baths, hydrotherapy and steam rooms all have been found beneficial in varying degrees. (*Ubogui J, et al. Thermalism in Argentina: alternative or complementary dermatologic therapy.* Archives of Dermatology. *1998;134:1411-1412.*)

Hypnosis /Self -Hypnosis

Hypnotherapy has been studied for decades and has a wide variety of medical and psychological applications. The effects and benefits of hypnosis go beyond the placebo effect and can be measured with brain imaging techniques. Dental and organ surgery, childbirth and other pain-inducing procedures have been performed while the patient was in a hypnosis-inducted analgesic trance. Self-esteem problems, addictions, and weight-loss are some of the many applications this powerful and well-documented complementary procedure. (*Friedman H, and Taub H. The use of hypnosis and biofeedback procedures for essential hypertension.* International Journal of Clinical and Experimental Hypnosis. *1977;25:335-347.*)

1. Very relaxing and never completely lose awareness during hypnosis
2. Can be done with eyes open or closed
3. Allows one to experience thoughts and images as real, so one willingly suspends disbelief for the moment
4. Elements of a trance
   a. Reduces muscular activity and energy output
   b. Rigidity of the muscles of the limbs
   c. Literal level of understanding
   d. Narrowing of attention
   e. Increased suggestibility

Imagery Desensitization

1. Most effective way to overcome a phobia is to face it. Avoidance keeps the phobia alive.
2. Sensitization is the process of becoming sensitized to a particular situation, and learning to associate anxiety with that situation.
3. Desensitization is the process of unlearning the connection between anxiety and a particular situation.
4. Imagery desensitization is when one visualizes being in a phobic situation while one is relaxed. If one begins to feel anxious, retreat from the imagined phobic situation and imagine oneself in a peaceful scene.
5. Steps:
   a. Deep state of relaxation for approximately 10-15 minutes.
   b. Begin with the individual's hierarchy of mild anxiety - provoking to very anxiety.
   c. Be vivid and use detail in the visualization of the anxiety-provoking scene and in the peaceful scene.
   d. Practice.

Inner Child Work

Divine child (Carl Jung), inner child; wonder child is the part of one that feels like a little girl or boy. This inner child feels and expresses our deepest emotional needs for security, trust, nurturing, affection, and touching. She or he is energetic, creative, playful and carries the pain and emotional trauma of our childhood. This is the child we once were who lives on, both in the positive aspects of the individual's personality and in old, self diminishing assumptions, attitudes and habitual behaviors. This is the part that thinks in catastrophic terms. Every criticism, loss, separation is a potential threat to its very existence. We tend to treat our inner child in much of the same way our parents treated us.

Working with Inner Child
1. Visualize (old photos help)
2. Just look at her or him—how old, what are they doing, what is their mood?
3. Begin to nurture, parent and be positive with her or him.
4. Talk in a calm, loving, supportive way. Never criticize the individual's child or demand that she or he shapes up.
5. Let her or him talk to one.

Journaling
1. Tracking subjective experience
2. Tracking discoveries which remediate anxiety

Lifestyle Changes
1) Decrease caffeine
2) Increase exercise
3) Vision, etc.
4) Practice non-avoidance
5) Observe and alter self-statements
6) Paradoxical Intention Verbalized
7) Assertiveness training
8) Self-esteem
9) Socialization and self-ownership

Light and Circadian Therapy

A significant number of individuals become depressed during the darker months of winter. Bright light therapy has been employed to remediate this effect with clinically significant results. Typically this light (2,500 to 10,000 lux) is applied for 20 minutes to 1 hour upon rising in the morning with the idea that this will "reset" circadian body rhythms. Some studies have argued against this circadian phase-delay hypothesis by finding that bright light can reduce the symptoms of SAD when applied during other times of the day. Endogenous melatonin levels correlate with light exposure and disregulated brain melatonin has been associated with psychological dysfunction and physical disease. Melatonin may hold the key for future research in this area. (*Wirz-Justic A, et al. Light therapy in seasonal affective disorder is independent of time of day or circadian phase.* Archives of General Psychiatry. *1993;50:929-937.*)

Magnetic Field Therapy

Clinical biomagnetics is an emerging science based on the interaction of living organisms with stable magnetic fields. Magnetic fields are classified in terms of their frequency of oscillation ranging from direct current (DC) and extremely low frequency (ELF) to gamma radiation. Oscillating, non-ionizing EM
fields in the ELF range can be created by the application of stationary magnets to the human body. Health benefits via increased blood flow, modification of cell membrane transport, and production of various chemical mediators have been measured empirically. Another type of magnetic therapy is called Rapid Rate Trans-Cranial Magnetic Stimulation (rTMS). Although used for years in diagnostic contexts, therapeutic uses for rTMS are still being researched and

the procedures are generally available only at major universities and medical centers. rTMS is used in a similar manner to Electro Convulsive Therapy (ECT) to treat depression, Attention Deficit Disorders, Parkinson's Disease and other neuropsychological problems.

Meditation

Meditation comes in many forms and represents many things to many people. In general mediation is a technique for focusing the mind on an object (e.g. a candle or flower) or activity (e.g. breathing) in order to quiet the body and the mind. During mediation the participant learns to gradually separate who they are as an individual from the thoughts that go on in their mind. This process is called "mindful awareness" and has been associated with both psychological and physiological health benefits. (*Kabat-Zinn J, et al. Influences of a mindfulness mediation-based stress reduction intervention on rate of skin clearing in patients with moderate to severe psoriasis undergoing phototherapy (UVB) and photochemotherpay (PUVA).* Psychosomatic Medicine. *1998;60:625-632.*)

1. There are several different types.
    a. Meditation is the practice of attempting to focus the individual's attention on one thing at a time.
    b. The "thing" is unimportant.
    c. The attempt to focus on one item is important, not the failures.
    d. When the mind drifts to other thoughts, dwell on the original object of attention.
2. Technique
    a. Requires a quiet environment
    b. Some type of mental device
    c. Comfortable position and a passive attitude
    d. Breathe through the nose. Place the tongue on the roof of the mouth
    e. Close the eyes and focus on the place where the body touches the cushion of the floor.
    f. Focus on how one breathes
    g. Passive attitude includes a lack of concern about whether one is doing things correctly. Instead, focus on "I'm going to put my time here, just sitting and whatever happens is exactly what should happen."
    h. Select a word or syllable like. "ONE" or the universal mantra "OM" and chant the word.
    i. Good to build up to 20 minutes a day

Music Therapy

Singing and music preceded speech and evolved as an elaboration of mating calls. Singing allowed our ancestors to transmit information over greater distances, affirm territorial boundaries, and attract groups and prepare them for action. In studios, music has been found to have a powerful influence on emotional processing and expression and to play an important role in social communication. (*Hanser S and Thompson L. Effects of music therapy strategy on depressed older adults.* Journal of Gerontology. *1994;49:265-269.*)

Negative Ion Therapy

Various brands of negative ion generators can be purchased to increase the negative ionization of indoor air. Creates similar feeling to being near waterfall or river. Research studies have shown a reduction in depression on exposure to high densities of negative ions.

Nutritional and Nutraceutical Consultation

Vitamin supplements, fat intake, fruits and vegetables and dozens of other nutritional elements have all been studied extensively in the peer-reviewed literature. Some suggestions for nutrition for anxiety reduction are included below:

1. Substances that aggravate anxiety
   a. Stimulants
   b. Nicotine
   c. Preservatives
   d. Stimulant drugs
   e. Salt
   f. Hormones in meat
2. Dietary Suggestions
   a. 5 or 6 small meals spaced three hours apart
   b. Eliminate as much "simple sugar" from the diet as possible
   c. Substitute fruits
   d. Reduce or eliminate simple starches such as pasta and white bread
   e. Eat more "natural" fruits and vegetables, and wash chemical residues away
   f. Decrease red meat intake. Increase fish.
3. Vitamins
   a. Deficiencies in Vitamin B1, B2, B6, and B12 can lead to anxiety, irritability, restlessness, fatigue and emotional instability.
   b. Vitamin C is depleted under stress
   c. Niacin (B3) B15, folic acid, choline, L-tryptophun, Vitamin A, beta carotene, chromium, inositol
4. Minerals
   a. Calcium and magnesium, silicon, multiple vitamin marganese
5. Foods that contain needed "vitamins" for anxiety
   a. B1 (thiamine)—whole grains, oatmeal, bran, most vegetables, peanuts, legumes and oranges.
   b. B2 (riboflavin)—spinach, dairy products, broccoli, green leafy vegetables, fish, eggs, and poultry.
   c. B3 (niacin)—tuna, chicken breasts, fortified breads, cereals, wheat germ, dates, figs, prunes, broccoli, tomatoes, and carrots.
   d. B5 (pantothenic acid)—mushrooms, salmon, soybeans, nuts, wheat germ, cantaloupe, bananas, peas, salmon and cod, clams, crab, tuna, salmon, oysters, dairy products, and tofu.

Here are some additional nutritional suggestions that support OCD recovery specifically:

- Stay away from alcohol altogether-or keep its use to a minimum. Minimum use might consist of a single beer or small glass of wine at any one time on special occasions, no more than 3-4 times in a month.

- Do not eat-refined carbohydrates or sugars in any form on an empty stomach (i.e., pasta, white breads, pastries, candy, jams, syrups, fruit juices, fruit, chocolate, alcohol).

- Eat three moderate sized nutritionally balanced meals each day. Avoid snacking: when one must choose wisely.
- Include vegetables or vegetable juices with at least two out of the individual's three meals a day
- Include a small amount of protein in the individual's diet-preferably from sources other than meat and poultry (soybean products, legumes, nuts, low-fat/nonfat dairy products in moderation)
- Use whole grains as main sources of carbohydrates
- Eat small-to-moderate amounts of fruit and unsalted unroasted nuts
- Reduce the individual's intake of fats.
- Use monounsaturated oils (extra light virgin olive oil, canola oil)
- Eliminate the following from the individual's diet, or cut down significantly: stimulants such as coffee, tea, cola drinks, chocolate, alcohol, high-cholesterol products such as bacon, red meats; high-fat dairy products; saturated fats (butter, shortening).
- When you're thirsty, drink water at room temperature instead of a soda.
- When you want a hot drink, drink herb teas, which contain no caffeine.
- Hot chamomile tea is especially recommended for its calming, soothing effects.
- Become a savvy, informed consumer of nutritional products

Oriental Medicine
Practiced by much of the world, oriental medicine approaches healthcare from a systemic perspective focusing on the relationship and balance between organs and systems. The emphasis in oriental medicine in on practices which can be performed from outside the body (e.g. acupuncture, moxibustion) and on herbs rather than surgical procedures. (*Cardini F and Weixin H. Moxibustion for correction of breech presentation.* Journal of the American Medical Association. *1998;280:1580-1584.*)

Phytomedicinal Supplements
* Inositol - (NOW Foods)
* Gamma-aminobutyric Acid (GABA)
* 5-hydroxy-L-tryptophane (5-HTP) – (Allergy Research 800-545-9960)
* Passion Flower – (Natures Way)
* Hypericum Perforatum (SJW) – (LI160 "Kira" by Litchwere Pharma)
* Kava Kava
* Omega-3
* B-Vitamins – (Solgar)

Vitamin B3 as niacinamide may be especially beneficial. It has been shown in animals to work in the brain in ways similar to drugs, such as Valium®, which are used to treat anxiety. One study found that niacinamide could help people get through withdrawal from Valium-type drugs-a common problem. A reasonable amount of niacinamide (not niacin) to take for anxiety, according to some doctors of natural medicine, is up to 500 mg four times per day.

*Hops – (Natures Way)

*Lemon Balm – (Natures Way)

Qigong (Chi Kung)

Used for thousands of years in oriental cultures to promote mental, emotional and physical balance. Particularly helpful with anxiety reduction and quieting the mind. An excellent "Qigong Healing Workout" video by Dr. Jerry Alan Johnson can purchased through China Healthways 800-743-5608.

Self Esteem Building

1. "Fake it 'til you makes it"
2. Counter negative statements
3. Look in the mirror everyday for five minutes and say, "I am okay". One has positive attributes (from the individual's list)
4. Use the individual's affirmations
5. Treat the OC sufferer the way one treats others
6. Pamper the OC sufferer but set boundaries
7. Honor the individual's needs

Sleep Hygiene

Sleep researchers have developed many different strategies for treating insomnia and hypersomnia conditions as well as disturbances such as nightmares, nocturnal myoclonus, and sleep-phase disorders. Many different suggestions are included at the end of this Key section. (*Hauri P, and Linde S.* No more sleepless nights. *New York, NY: John Wiley and Sons; 1990.*)

Spirituality

Clinical and epidemiological studies have demonstrated a causal relationship between individual and group spirituality and various desirable health effects. People with strong spiritual beliefs tend to live longer and healthier lives than their non-spiritual peers regardless of denominational affiliation. (*Oxman T, et al.*
Lack of social participation or religious strength and comfort as risk factors for death after cardiac surgery in the elderly. Psychosomatic Medicine. *1995;57:681-689.*)

Stress Management

When humans are under the threat of real or perceived life stress, the sympathetic nervous system becomes highly active resulting in accelerating heartbeat, adrenaline secretion, a decrease in digestive functions and numerous other physiologic effects. Prolonged periods of sympathetic nervous system arousal have been associated with a wide range of disorders from allergies and asthma to warts and yeast infection. Specific life management skills enable the individual to rebalance parasympathetic and sympathetic nervous system responses. Some common ways of reducing stress are:

- Decrease expectations
- Decrease life change
- Follow common routines
- Reduce life stressors
- Increase sense of control

(*Farsure-Smith N. In hospital symptoms of psychological stress as predictors of long-term outcome after acute myocardial infarction in men.* American Journal of Cardiology. *1991;67:121-27.*)

Stroebel's Quieting Reflex

1. Be aware of the stimulus one is responding to (loud noises, crowded places, etc,)
2. Give the OC sufferer the suggestion "Alert mind, calm body." The idea is to pause and use the inner freedom.
3. Smile inwardly with the eyes and mouth to reverse their tendency to go into a grim set.
4. Inhale slowly and easily to a count of two, three, or four, imagining the breath coming in through the pores in the bottom of the feet. A feeling of "flowing warmth and flowing heaviness coming up through the middle of the legs" may accompany this mental image. As one exhales, let the jaw, tongue and shoulders go limp. Feeling the wave of heaviness and warmth flowing to the toes. Then resume normal activity.

Support Groups

Whether one is part of a formal "support group" or an informal circle of friends, or colleagues' social interaction is a valuable part of healthcare. Empirical research has shown causal links between increased levels of social support and more rapid recovery from illness and surgery, lower blood pressure, increased longevity. Being in healthy relationships (even with pets and plants) can provide psychological defense again adverse life events. Caring for others has been associated with lower levels of psychological depression. (*Cohen S and Syme S eds.* Social Support and Health. *New York, NY; Academic Press; 1985.*)

The Ten-Second Grip

1. Grab and squeeze the armrest of the chair, tensing the upper and lower arms. Tense the stomach and leg muscles as well. Hold that position about 10 seconds while one continues to breathe.
2. Let go and take a Calming Breath.
3. Repeat two more times.
4. Shift around in the seat, shaking loose the arms, shoulders, and legs, and gently rolling the head a few times.
5. Close the eyes and breathe gently for about 30 seconds. Let the body feel warm, relaxed, and heavy during that time.

Toning

1. Repeat "Ahhh…" for five minutes.

Thought Stopping

1. Thought stopping involves concentrating on the unwanted thoughts and after a short time, suddenly stopping and emptying the mind.

    a. The command "stop" or a loud noise is used to interrupt the unpleasant thought.

    b. Effective with a variety of obsessive and phobic thought processes. 70% against phobias.

    c. For mastery, thought stopping must be practiced consistently throughout the day for 3-5 days.

    d. Good for worriers.

2. How to complete thought stopping:

    a. List five thoughts which are unnecessary, interfering, compulsive, or intrusive.

    b. Imagine the thought. Close the eyes and bring into imagination where the stressful thoughts are likely to occur.

    c. Interrupt the thought. Shout, Stop, or hear the word shouted in the head.

    d. Substitute a thought. Replace thought with a positive assertive statement. Have several for each unwanted thought.

    e. May use a rubber band that one snaps instead of shouting out loud "STOP"

    f. Takes time to practice

Uncover Past Learning ("Scripting")
1. Security/insecurity at home
2. Abandonment fear
3. Family HX of anxiety

Yoga and Martial Arts

Various forms of yoga, tai chi chuan, aikido and other "internal" martial arts lend themselves well to psycho physiological healthcare. Often these interventions are mistakenly associated with religious practices when in fact they were generally designed as medicinal, meditative, or self-defense disciplines. Gastrointestinal disorders, allergies, migraine headache, anxiety, rheumatoid conditions, and other states of disease may be assisted by participation in yogic and martial training programs. (*Garfinkel S, et al. Yoga-based intervention for carpal tunnel syndrome.* Journal of the American Medical Association. *1998;280:1601-1603.*)

OVERVIEW OF OC TREATMENT TECHNIQUES

<u>"Anxiety Disorders"</u>

Obsessive-Compulsive Disorder: Invitro and in vivo exposure and response prevention (ERP); Massed exposure; Anxiety management techniques; Obsession inoculation; Cognitive therapy.

<u>"Impulse Control Disorders"</u>

Trichotillomania: Awareness and habit reversal training; Relaxation response techniques.

<u>"Somatoform Disorders"</u>

Hypochondriasis: Obsession inoculation; Exposure and response prevention; Attention training; Relaxation response training; Cognitive-behavioral therapy

Body Dysmorphic Disorder: Invitro and in vivo exposure and response prevention (ERP); Massed exposure; Anxiety management techniques; Obsession inoculation; Cognitive therapy; Family therapy

<u>"Disorders First Diagnosed in Childhood"</u>

Tourette's Disorder: Habit reversal training; Sensory integration training

Stereotypic Movement Disorders: Habit reversal training.

Aspergers Syndrome Shifting attention; Obsession inoculation; Relationship skills; Expanding range of interest; Sensory integration; Emotional management.

DEVELOPING COGNITIVE RESTRUCTURING & OBSESSION-INNOCULATION STRATEGIES

- *Approximately one quarter* of OCD sufferers has what is considered Primarily Obsessional" OCD of O-OCD (e.g. obsessions are predominant with few or even no compulsive or ritual behaviors that attend them.)

- Compulsions are the part of Obsessive-compulsive Disorder that receives the most attention from researchers to the media. On the other hand it is the obsessive mode of thought that links all OC-spectrum disorders together as a family.

- Two parts: (1) the original *unwanted thought* and (2) the *mental ritualizing* or obsessing that attempts to "undue" the unwanted thought.

- In OC language, unwanted intrusive thoughts are often referred to as *"hits" or "spikes"*.

- May go down dozens of obsessive *"rabbit holes"* every day – becoming "stuck" and ruminating over aspects of relationships, work, self-image, diet and exercise, personal hygiene, even a dream from the previous night.

- If the thought has *anxiety attached*, or if the individual becomes anxious when asked to not counter the thought with a ritual or mental compulsion, then the thought is very likely an expression of OCD.

- Like mental *quicksand*. The more the OC sufferer thinks about them and tries to fight the way out by force of mental effort the more he or she will become stuck in them. Relaxing is much better medicine than tightening up and worrying that the obsessing will never stop.

- "One Second Rule".

THE ONE SECOND RULE

- *Though-action fusion* versus delusion.

- The *longer the thought is dwelled on*, the more the brain says "Hey, this must be important! I will set aside lots of file space and focus on this more!"

- Secondary thought loops. (1) See knife in kitchen – (2) Unwanted thought of stabbing loved one – (3) *"I must be a terrible, disgusting person to think such a thought"* or (1) Thought of "I should have more friends" – (2) Tensing up and focusing inward (3) *"I won't be OK until I have more friends."*

- Sometimes obsessions can be the result of difficulties with memory (e.g. obsessing about what signs say, or if the stove is turned off). Explore if this might be the case for the individual. If so, develop *memory tools* to assist the individual.

- Most obsessions have in them at least a *potential kernel of reality.*
  Examples: Hurting child
  Hearing being damaged by a loud noise
  Eyes damaged by sunlight

- Three general levels or types: *Common, Global and Intrusive.*

Common Obsessions are those that tend to pop up as part of daily living ("Did I just get glass in my eye from that jar that my spouse dropped in the other room when I was not even around?") Similar to Type II Diabetes, Common Obsessions cause discomfort, but usually not disability and are usually manageable through obsession inoculation techniques.

Global Obsessions are those pervasive, consuming, life-infringing obsessions that are usually highly disturbing to the individual and make it difficult to function in work, relationships and self-care. Global Obsessions are often frightening and disturbing and many times center around such issues as religion, harming others, sexuality, bodily injury, or timeline distortions.

Intrusive Obsessions are less common and often very difficult to remove. Examples of Intrusive Obsessions include songs, noises, images, or phrases that replay over and over in the sufferer's mind and seem impossible to shut off. It is as if the individual's mind becomes caught in an endless feedback loop.

- Start the treatment process by writing down the obsessions in *list form,* rating their intensity, listing what comes before the obsession ("trigger".) and what comes after the obsession ("neutralizing strategy".)

- The second main task is to *habituate* to the obsession.

- Active treatment for obsessional OCD should not be attempted until the individual is *fully committed* to do whatever it takes to fight off the OCD.

- Unlike C-OCD, it is usually necessary to *jump right into the worst* of the obsessions and give them no quarter to escape and regroup.

- *Defensive strategies*, attempts to gain reassurance, or seeking comfort from the obsessions invariably causes them to escalate.

- Exposure and Response Prevention (ERP) behavioral treatment is like an *immunization*.

- It is also **crucial** to remember that:
    - Obsession-based OCD takes six to twelve months or more to treat to any significant degree and
    - The number of "hits" or attacks by the obsession (e.g. the frequency with which the obsession presents itself into consciousness) will almost always *increase* during the first weeks and months of treatment.
    - Goal of treatment is not a decrease in hits, but rather a *decrease in the amount of time and intensity* with which the individual dwells on, or gets stuck in the obsession.

- *NEUTRALIZATION* **is an essential concept in understanding obsessions:**

- ***Neutralization Defined: Any mental or physical action, regardless of form, performed for the goal of controlling or removing anxiety or an anxiety provoking thought (obsession), changing its meaning, preventing negative consequences, or forestalling future occurrences of the thought.***

- One of the difficulties in identifying patient's neutralization behaviors is that neutralization behaviors can be so subtle.

    Types of neutralizing thoughts expressed by an individual include:
    (1) Assessment,
    (2) Experience,
    (3) Spontaneous,
    (4) Triggered,

- Triggers for neutralization's can be either external or internal and there's a great degree of variation.

- If it's effortful it has become part of the problem.

- There's a great deal of variation in the amount of neutralization which obsessive compulsive patients experience. Factors which determines neutralization include;
    (1) Mood,
    (2) Fatigue,
    (3) Stress,
    (4) Life events,

(5) Seasonal patterns,
(6) Weekends vs. weekdays,
(7) Activity level, and even
(8) Hormonal variations for females.

- About 50 percent of patients with OCD will use ritualized cognitions in order to neutralize.

- On average the obsessive compulsive individual has at least 10 to 40 neutralization strategies which they employed at various times and various situations.

- Neutralization's can include reassurance seeking from others. An easy way to identify reassurance seeking is if questions are asked repetitively.

- It is also important to remember that avoidance can be a form of neutralization. Can have Obsessions not be bothered by them because they've been able to structure life around the sessions.

- Can't control many events in life including: Mood, triggers, physiology, life events. Can however, control the importance which they attach to their thoughts about these events.

- Any treatment strategies which do not involve a confrontation between the patient and their anxiety are unlikely to succeed. (E.g. guided imagery strategies where the individual visualizes putting their obsessive thought in a balloon.)

- Careful about responding to reassurance seeking behavior. Answer a new question one time. Ask patient to write their question down and hold onto it for a week. Then they can decide if the question is still is important to them.

- One main aim is to allow the patient to simply be with a thought. To stand there in the presence of the anxiety provoking thought while it washes over them anticipates leaving in its wake positive brain change.

OBSESSION-INNOCULATION STRATEGIES

- Learning to *tolerate* the unwanted thoughts and simply *feel the anxiety* is the primary goal of O-OCD treatment.

- *Multi-Sensory Massed Imaginal Exposure (MSME).* This is the primary and, usually, most powerful technique for working through primarily obsessive OCD. Should not be used where psychosis or antisocial features are present.

- *Encouraging the Obsession.* Must be done primarily in the original medium of the obsession.

  - Other methods of encouraging the obsession include:
    - Writing out or saying the feared thoughts, acts, statements or sentences
    - Reading books, watching a video, or making a scrapbook about the obsession
    - Deliberately going places where one will encounter the obsession
    - Taking part in feared activities
    - Resisting doing things the obsession says one must do
    - Making a card, t-shirt or other expression of the obsession

- *Discontinue, as much as possible, reassurance seeking.* Note that reassurance seeking and neutralizing behaviors can be very subtle.

- *Break the rules.* The individual may find creative ways to challenge the obsessive thought. For example:
  - Change the obsessive thought by adding an element in the middle or they may cut the thought off half-way.
  - Delaying the obsessive thought or acting it out in pantomime very, very slowly.

- *Include the family.* Having a loved one participate in the treatment process (without providing unhealthy reassurance or enmeshing with the individual) increases the chances of treatment.

- *Attention Training (ATT).* Attention Training is the primary tool used at the OCD Recovery Center for assisting OC sufferers in detaching from obsessive thoughts and reducing overvalued ideation. Deveed by British researcher Adrian Wells.and involves

- *Meditation* is an alternative for those who do not benefit from, or dislike Attention Training. Realizing that obsessions are of no real consequence helps to see them as "just brain noise" – the result of disordered impulses coming from the brain.

- *Maintaining a healthy stress/relaxation balance* is critical in recovery from O-OCD.

- *Yoga Breathing.* Researchers at UCLA developed and tested a yoga breathing technique which reportedly reduced some forms of OCD by 70% or more. Closing off the right nostril and breathing through the left (both inhalation and exhalation) for approximately 30 minutes per day. The positive effects were seen over six to twelve months of daily practice.

- *Centering.* The primary skill needed to transcend obsessions is to shift the individual's *focus inward* (through centering, physical techniques, etc.) and then actively *relax*.

- View anxiety as the fuel that causes obsessions to appear. Developing *active methods for anxiety reduction* tends to reduce obsession in general

- *Attempting to suppress thoughts* almost always has the opposite of the intended effect – making them stronger still. Thought stopping and other similar techniques done with this for this purpose tend to be counterproductive.

- For Intrusive Obsessions creating *brief exposures* (e.g. turning off and on the part of a song that gets stuck in the individual's mind) may be helpful.

- *Neurofeedback* is another emerging tool for confronting obsessions. Neurofeedback is done with a highly trained psychologist who first makes a "brain map" of the individual using computerized electroencephalograph equipment.

- Obsessions are "projections" of the self into the past, the future, other people, etc. *Focusing on the present* and what the individual is doing right this moment diminishes the hold obsessions have.

- *Humor.* Is very important in obsession recovery. OCD wants the sufferer to take it seriously. Finding ways to make fun of the obsession ("And now Dr. Evil is going to kill.")

- Focusing the mind on *positive circumstances* or behaviors rather than the obsessions or what might be "wrong" tends to decrease some obsessions. A good way of doing this is by making a "gratitude list".

- Encourage a *"Just be and don't think"* attitude on a continual basis. Obsessions live in the mind. Redirecting the attention always back on experience versus thoughts helps calm down obsessions.

- *Shadowing.* Following someone the individual trusts through a behavior that has been difficult due to obsessing can help to break the obsessive routine or rut.

- *Obsession Box.* Place a copy of the Serenity Prayer on a box or bag. The individual can then write down an obsession, place it in the box, then let it go mentally.

- *Thought Backtracking.* What was the thought they had before the current one? What was the one before that? What was the initial thought ("engine") that started off the thought train? When the sufferer arrives back to the original thought – almost always something involving the material world, five senses and real, present-time experience, instruct them to stop and focus on enjoying that.

- *Slow Motion Focus.* If the individual tends to become stuck in a particular behavior it may be helpful to try going very, very slowly through the behavior. For example: Put in the key…wait…turn the key…wait…pull the key out…wait…turn the knob slowly…wait…open the door slowly.

- For individuals having trouble getting free of an obsession, have them try *changing the setting.*

- To combat obsessions it is helpful to take some time each day to *practice "Non-doing".*

- *Saying "No"* to "shoulds" tends to lead the mind away from obsessions. Help the individual to find their *"want to".*

- *Ritual Delay.* This involves delaying acting out a compulsion, which will reduce the individual's anxiety about an obsession. Example: wait 60 minutes before doing a neutralizing ritual.

- Keep in mind the idea of an *"Obsession Pie".* Visualize a pie with a very small slice darkened in. This slice represents the reality of the individual's worries – most worries have at least some basis in reality. The rest of the pie represents obsession. The job is to reduce the obsession part of the pie.

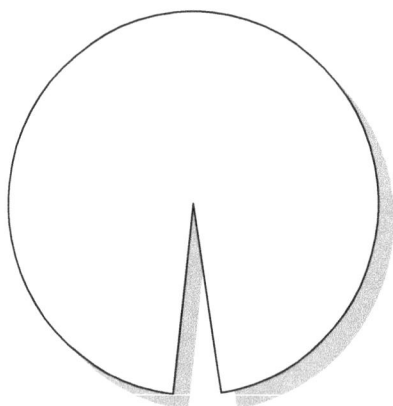

OBSESSION VERSUS REALITY

- *Ah…* Every word the human race has created for "God" has the sound *"ah"* in it. Making this sound creates a pleasant and anxiety reducing vibration in the body.

- *Compulsion Substitution.* In an emergency, instead of the individuals' usual obsession - try (for example) substituting tapping gently three times on the head. Let this satisfy the OCD for the time being until other tools for recovery can be developed. (Will probably encourage the obsessions when used.)

- *Encourage a sympathetic self-view.* Having an obsessive-compulsive disorder is difficult, stressful and time consuming. Remind the individual not to expect themselves to be able to accomplish what they could if they did not have a disability. Encourage them to be understanding and to take it easy on themselves.

- *The Head Shake Technique.* If the individual finds themselves obsessing suggest they simply shake their head as if shaking the thought right out of their head.

- Encourage the individual to keep in mind some *helpful slogans* and reminders such as: "Relax." "De-escalate." "Disinhibit." "Be spontaneous." "Detach." "Let go." "Accept." "It's ok to have things be imperfect." "Lighten up!" "Say "So what!". "Live in the now."

- Reduce one's general anxiety level and, or avoid situations which create anxiety.

- The oriental practice of Qigong is very helpful in reducing the anxiety and providing a healthy activity to do while experiencing the anxiety related to ERP work.

- *Neutralization obsessions* involve the replaying in the individual's mind of an anxiety-producing event. Although this may look like obsessing it can actually be a form of self-stimulation. Neutralization obsessions call for a "letting go" approach in which they are encouraged to simply let the thoughts flow through them without hindrance.

- *Catharsis can be illusion.* One of the difficulties for individuals with obsessional thinking is that it is difficult to trust one's own ideas and feelings. Many times it becomes important to set limits on "self-exploration" (e.g. delving into childhood trauma) because the obsessive ideation is distorting the situation out of proportion. (EMDR) works well for this purpose (although people with OCD often respond differently to EMDR than other subjects). For people with OCD, feelings can be more of an illusion than an answer.

BEHAVIOR THERAPY FOR OBSESSIVE COMPULSIVE DISORDERS

- Builds on treatment strategies for Obsession Inoculation.

- Behavior therapy, and specifically "exposure and response prevention" (ERP) therapy shown consistently, since the mid-1970's, to be the most effective method of treating OCD.

- Overvalued ideation - the belief that the anxiety is rational. Behavior therapy is contraindicated or difficult. Use cognitive therapy to demonstrate that the fear is not rational. Group therapy also helpful.

- *Depression* also a poor prognostic factor. Consider using medication.

- ERP can be combined with imaginal flooding, participant modeling, massed exposure, or progressive or rapid desensitization.

- Behavior therapy begins with the exhaustive identification of core OCD behaviors including type, frequency, attempts to resist the obsessions and compulsions.

- Identify fears hidden behind others such as the common fear that by not performing a ritual the obsession will magically *follow the OC sufferer into the future* via ruminations which cannot now be undone.

- Write out what they believe will happen if they come in contact with the feared object or situation and carefully compose "obsession statements" based on identified fears.

- Identify factors of secondary gain, if any are important in the development of an exposure and response prevention plan.

- Evaluate the need to discharge anxiety through reassurance seeking behavior.

- Rank-order a list of compulsions or rituals with subjective units of distress (SUDS). (Including avoided situations, people, etc.) Each situation is given point value from 0 – 100 - No Anxiety (0) to Medium Anxiety (50) to Extreme Anxiety (100).

- May be necessary to spend time deliberately developing an experiential sense for the individual's personal anxiety symptoms.

- Starting with a mid-range anxiety-provoking situation and begins to direct exposure to the obsessed stimuli while visualizing the most feared consequences of not ritualizing.

- When conducting ERP the OC sufferer should avoid reducing anxiety and instead embrace or welcome it with intent to allow it to "burn off".

THE FIVE CRITICAL ELEMENTS OF OC TREATMENT

I.   **SAFETY**– A slice of the pie is reality, but 99% is obsession

II.   **INTENSITY** - keeping anxiety levels between the SUD levels of 25-75
   - Too Many
   - Too Large

III.   **NEUTRALIZATION** – make sure the OC sufferer does not "undue" the exposure with rituals or compulsions. (Sometimes OC sufferers have been known to "hold out" for weeks or months before performing a compulsion or ritual to "make it better" and thus neutralize the ERP work!)

IV. **SATURATION** – making the exposure constantly present
   - Commitment
   - Habituation

V.   **DURATION** – holding the exposure for as long as it takes to habituate

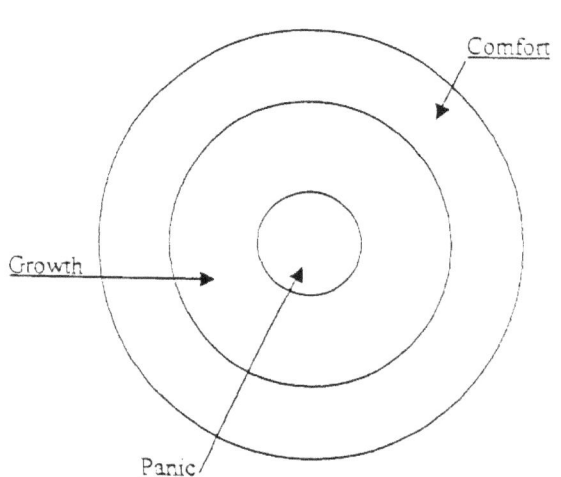

Habitation

"The elimination of a response as a result of continuous exposure to the stimulus which evoked the response."

VS.

Desensitization

"Weakening of a response with repeated presentation of the stimulus."

Habituation is more similar to behavioral flooding than desensitization (like with fear of flying).

70

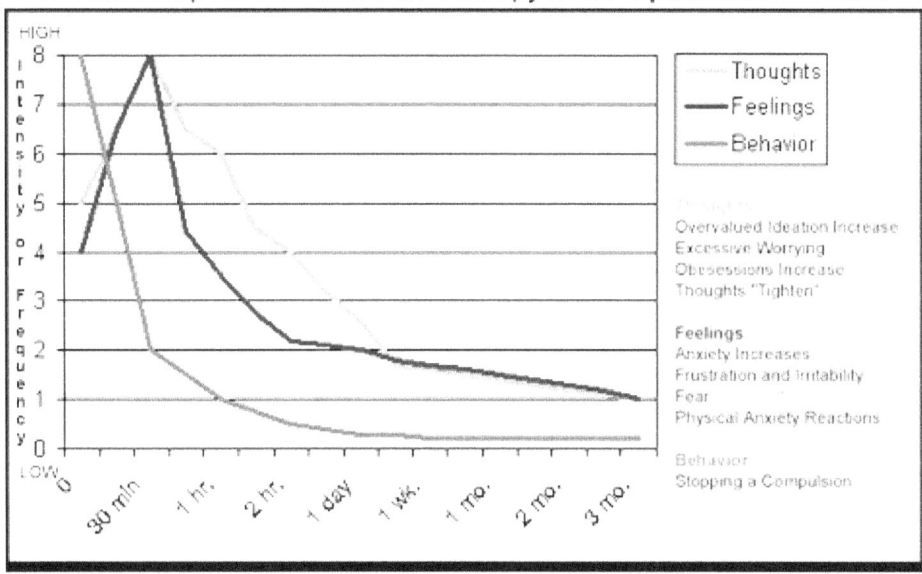

Normal Response To Behavior Therapy In OC-Spectrum Disorders

THE SEVEN STEPS FOR FIGHTING OCD

STEP ONE: SELECT THE *INTENSITY*
- ➤ Only rituals achieving a rating of 25-75 are selected for ERP.
- ➤ Danger in selecting items with SUDs rating over 75 are: *Panic and Neutralization*

STEP TWO: INITIATE *RESISTANCE*
- ➤ A ritual is selected for elimination
- ➤ Individual refuses to perform the ritual behavior or thought in spite of the urgings of the OC disorder.
- ➤ Done with an awareness that the surge of anxiety experienced when refusing a ritual will dissipate within minutes to hours (often in 15 to 20 minutes).

STEP THREE: PAUSE, SEE, *RENAME*
- ➤ The urge to perform the obsessive ritual is in reality a faulty brain message.
- ➤ *Stopping all activity* and concentrating one's awareness on what's happening - on the obsession or ritual - long enough to *truly and clearly see and feel* it is just OCD and not a "real" danger or issue.
- ➤ Slogans and other forms of self-talk can be used to achieve this end.
- ➤ Have a working awareness of one's mental, physical, and emotional symptoms of anxiety. Say, "This is just anxiety caused by the obsession or compulsion I am refusing to give in to."

STEP FOUR: *REFOCUS* ATTENTION
- ➤ Not necessary to obsessively focus on the anxiety that is naturally generate.
- ➤ Be aware of the anxiety, to see it for what it is (Step Three).
- ➤ Do something else – go on with life as it were *carrying the anxiety with one*.

STEP FIVE: PRACTICE *TRUST*
- ➤ Develop trust in a higher power, the universe, destiny of life itself.
- ➤ *Serenity Prayer* exemplifies this Step: "Grant me the serenity to accept the things I cannot change, the courage to change the things I can and the *wisdom* to know the difference."
- ➤ Remember that compulsive rituals are designed to try to control what cannot be controlled.

STEP SIX: *PERSIST* (50% Rule)
- ➤ Persist in refusing the ritual until the anxiety dissipates – however long this may take.
- ➤ Observing the anxiety level decreasing provides strong encouragement.

STEP SEVEN: *MAINTAIN* - DON'T UNDUE
- ➤ Once the anxiety does begin to reduce it is essential to avoid the temptation to perform another ritual to "undue" the curse of the first.

ADDITIONAL BEHAVIORAL THERAPY POINTS

- If one gives in to an OC ritual it is still possible to make it a "win" by clearly *acknowledging that one has had a "slip,"* and that the OC has won, but that nothing real has been accomplished.

- Important to maintain exposure, or at least awareness of the exposure, until anxiety level has gone *down by at least 50%* from its peak at the start of the exposure.

- Anxiety "burn off" process may take *minutes to hours*.

- Habituation *may take many months* to complete.

- Rating the anxiety on a 0-100 scale *every ten minutes* keeps the OC sufferer's attention on the process and serves to reinforce that the habituation process is taking place.

- Much of the work of the behavior therapist is in assisting the OC sufferer in grading, or *titrating the exposure*. This often requires a great deal of cleverness and ingenuity.

- The therapist or **recovery sponsor** can *model behavior* if needed.

- Once the individual's SUDS rating for the situation being worked on goes down by *50% and is 30 or below for two consecutive practice sessions,* one can move on to the next highest rated item on the exposure list.

- Prevent relapse by ensuring that if one "slips" and gives in to a compulsion or obsession, the individual's *counters the slip with a deliberate exposure in kind*.

- Use the *meditations, slogans and affirmations* (such as those found in The Obsessive-Compulsive's Meditation Book (2000) to get through times when ERP work, or in the course of life in general, anxiety has risen within the target zone of 25-75 points.

- "The time to build a roof on the house is when it is not raining." *ERP work should be daily, consistent and gradual* rather than sudden, unexpected or heroic.

- Don't focus on *feelings of doubt* ("What if..!"). See OC thoughts as "just brain noise".

- Try *"holding" the exposure in an experiential way* – for example by holding a cotton ball or tissue in the individual's hand to symbolize this while one is holding the anxiety regarding the exposure in the individual's awareness.

- *Anxiety must occur* for there to be a treatment benefit.

- Can work with *treatment buddy* to ensure compliance. Can gradually "fade" use of therapist or buddy.

- Use *imaginal exposure* with fears one can't really do in vitro (e.g. fear of death) or one can use "approximation" (go to cemetery)

- Can't do exposure without *response prevention* or response prevention without exposure.

- If the OC sufferer will not do response prevention - sit with them and supervise.

- Do not allow *replacement rituals*. ID what they are for each client.

- Don't allow *inadvertent checking, repeating, or ritualizing*. Get OC sufferer out of area so they can't do it!

- Teach what is *normal*.

- Don't allow more than *normal time or frequency* for activities. (e.g. not washing for 5 minutes)

- Thought stoppage is useful for *mental rituals* only.

- Make sure to *warn the OC sufferer* that recovery will take time and practice.

- Use *humor* whenever possible

- In vivo Situations: trigger anxiety by having the OC sufferer carry knife or sleep with it under bed. etc.

- In vivo treatment approaches are *more powerful* than in vitro or imaginal.

- If the OC sufferer is cooperating with therapy and yet does not improve *increase the frequency, duration, or intensity of the stimulation*.

- *The only reassurance* that should be offered is that "the anxiety will go down".

- Analogies can be helpful:

  o Fighting OCD is like climbing a ladder. One starts on the bottom rung.
  o Use a loosely and a tightly woven *net* to demonstrate obsessional mind.
  o OCD is like a giant loudspeaker in the brain. It broadcasts thoughts that should be quiet and unimportant in a VERY LOUD VOICE!
  o Habituation: If one goes in a cold lake and stays long enough one gets used to it.
  o Take the fear temperature and watch it go down during the exposure.
  o Pick up the individual's brain and put it where one wants it to be.

- Have the patient do something they *enjoy* while waiting for the fear to go down.

- Do an *OCD progress chart*. Draw the size of OCD each day or week. Encourage journal keeping.

- Remember, *the individual is not weird*. OCD is.

- Develop a *reward system* for good progress.

- Expert consensus is to *always use CBT first and then medication* if no response in 4-6 weeks.

- Medication "*turns down the volume*" of the OCD loudspeaker.

- Can do a *second 0-20 minute set* if fear is not down yet.

- As OCD gets larger the *safe zone gets smaller*. It's like "dancing on the head of a pin".

- Progress will not be steady. *Expect setbacks.*

- Know about *extinction bursts* that occur when one first works on a behavior.

- Expect the individual's work or school to provide "*accommodation*" as for any disability.

HOME-BASED "RECOVERY BUDDY" SYSTEM
FOR OC DISORDERS

* NOTE: Keep things simple and straightforward. Speak clearly, calmly, caringly. Keep the situation as positive as possible. Use humor as much as possible without making fun of the person. Realize anxiety levels related to obsessions can be tremendously high. There should only be one "Recovery Buddy" otherwise confusion can result. Remember the keys to OC recovery success: *Intensity, Saturation, Duration, and Neutralization.* Follow a pattern for working through the episode each time following the 10 steps that follow:

(1) Event or situation occurs.

(2) Ask if the person would like assistance or support. If yes…

(3) Assist them in determining how much of what they are experiencing is an obsession.

(4) Remind them this is a brain disorder and not "real" or their "fault".

(5) Ask them if they would like to challenge the obsession this time. This decision should be based on how much is already on the person's plate. (If they are highly stressed or coping with several other exposure situations already they may want to pass on this current challenge or wait until another time to confront the situation.)

(6) Ask how the person thinks they could best challenge the OC this time while staying in the 25-75 anxiety range. ("What would your counselor suggest?") Help them to figure out how to tone down or increase the anxiety level by modifying how they confront the OC (e.g. touching the normally avoided light switch with a Kleenex if bare hands would be a 90+ or with bare hands if using a tissue would be a 10-.)

(7) Ask the individual how they might normally neutralize or avoid the anxiety (e.g. saying a special prayer for safety) and then encourage them to avoid those activities.

(8) Remind the person to feel the anxiety flow through them while going on with the next set of normal activities of living.

(9) Remind the person to take their "fear temperature" every ten minutes once they start the exposure. Reassure them that the anxiety will go down.

(10) Avoid answering questions or requests for reassurance other than: (a) Confirming that this is OCD, (b) Confirming what "normal people" would do in this situation, (c) Reminding the person that the anxiety will go down if they stick with it, (d) For reassurance seeking remind them "You already know the answer".

HEALING RELATIONSHIPS IN OC RECOVERY

- Examine the relationships currently in the individual's life and those one might have an opportunity to enter into in the future. Set a goal of having at least one person in each of the relationship categories below. If one has lots of people in one category and only one in another investigate why this is and take steps to balance things out.
    - Family of Choice – Folks we invite into our inner circle with which we can be highly vulnerable and show all parts of our self. This is usually a small group of people.
    - Close Friends – People we interact with regularly. We may not share everything with them, but we feel we can turn to them in times of trouble or emergency and receive support. This group generally will contain as few as one and as many as five people.
    - Limited Friends – People who are not quite as close as the last group, but still folks we would go out of our way to be of service to or participate closely with in activities.
    - Acquaintances and Associates – Individuals with whom we have common interests including business. We recognize and enjoy each other's company, but would not necessarily turn to each other in times of crisis or need.
    - Esteem Builders – Could be members of any of the above groupings. These people believe in us and our abilities and can affirm us for our self-worth.
    - Cheerleaders – These are friends who encourage us and remind us of our power. They boost our spirits in tough times.
    - Advisors – These are people we can trust to guide us when we need advice. We empower them to give us "tough love" sometimes when we need it.
    - Feed backers – People who will tell us the truth even if it is not what we want to hear.

You do not need to leave your room.
Remain sitting at your table and listen.
Do not even listen, simply wait.
Do not even wait, be quite still and solitary.
The world will freely offer itself to one to be unmasked.
It has no choice, it will roll in ecstasy at your feet.
- Franz Kafka

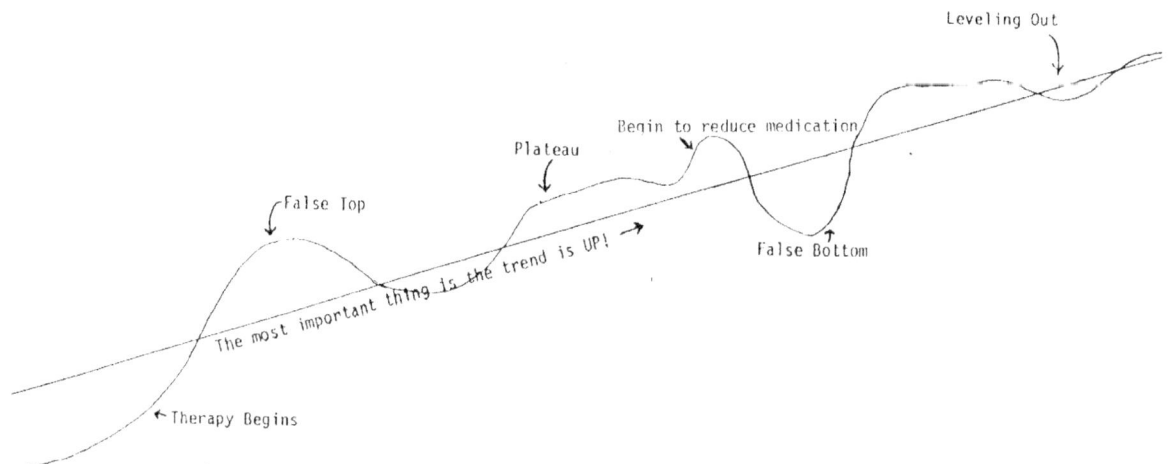

PROGRESS IN OCD AND RELATED DISORDERS
RECOVERY

MASTER OCD RECOVERY PLAN – PAGE I

SYMPTOM HIERARCHY   CHART OF OBSESSIONAL SYSTEM

OTHER CHARTS AND GRAPHS

MASTER OCD RECOVERY PLAN – PAGE II

AWARENESS

MOTIVATORS	OBSESSIONS
TRIGGERS/CYCLES	COMPULSIONS
STRESSORS	NEUTRALIZERS
PHYCHOLOGICAL LINKS	ANXIETY SYMPTOMS

TOOLS

EXPOSURE AND RESPONSE PREVENTION
  (1) Intensity - keeping anxiety levels between the SUB levels of 25-75
  (2) Saturation –making the exposure constantly present in the individual's environment,
  (3) Duration – holding the exposure for as long as it takes to habituate,
  (4) Neutralization – making sure the OC sufferer does not "undue" the exposure with rituals or compulsions. (Sometimes OC sufferers have been known to "hold out" for weeks or months before performing a compulsion or ritual to "make it better" and thus neutralize the ERP work!)

PERSPECTIVE, CONCEPTS AND COGNITIVE THERAPY

SELF-CARE PRACTICES AND PROCEEDURES

SUPPORTIVE RESOURCES AND AUGMENTATION AGENTS

EMERGENCY PLAN

AFTERWORD

LIFE IS LIKE A BIG CRANE GRAB GAME AT THE ARCADE
AND WE HAVE A CERTAIN AMOUNT OF TIME
– LIKE 15 SECONDS.
IT'S ACTUALLY SO YOU CAN HAVE FUN. THERE IS TIME IN OUR
GAME TO HAVE FUN AND WE NEED TO USE THE TIME IN OUR
LIFE TO DO THE THINGS WE NEED TO DO!

-Thomas R. Komor (Age 7 – First Grade)

EXPERIENCING OBSESSIVE COMPULSIVE DISORDERS AN ADVENTURE

CONTAMINATION OCD
. Do not enter a public bathroom.
. Do not directly touch any item that may have been touched by someone else. . Do not take or accept the top plate, cup, or any other item related to eating.

REPEATING AND SYMMETRY OCD
. Every time you pass a door, partition, overhang, crack or corner or make a significant action (taking money out, turning on faucet, picking up utensil, clicking open pen) think as you do so of the most terrible way you can imagine to die. Go back and repeat the pass thinking a "good thought" (happy vacation, loved one, etc.). Do not move forward until you have done so.
. If you notice a picture, ashtray, coaster, chair, rug or any item that is not perfectly lined up with its surroundings make sure to straighten it. Then straighten it a second time.

BODY DYSMORPHIC DISORDER
. You nose and eyebrows are hideously misshapen and everyone around you knows it, but won't say anything. Be constantly aware of your nose and eyebrows.
. Hide your nose and eyebrows as much as you can. Find creative ways to do this.

HOARDING OCD
. Read every printed word that falls within your vision.
. Write down or remember every proper name you hear of see.
. Save all paper items that you encounter even if it means embarrassing yourself

PURE-OBSESSION OF DANGEROUSNESS
. Every time you look at another person (including children) *visualize* a horrible way to kill them. Try not to use the same method twice.
. Do not go within lunging distance of any other human so that you will not be tempted to harm them.

TOURETTES DISORDER
. At the end of every other statement "cluck" tongue at least three times.
. Do not make eye contact under any circumstances.
. At least once every five minutes raise fist to waist and then drive straight down four times.

HYPOCHONDRIASIS
. Find a bathroom and check your torso, armpits, groin, and neck for suspicious lumps.
. Be constantly aware of your heartbeat and notice any irregularities. Take your pulse at least every ten minutes.
. Confine all conversations to health-related topics. Ask continual questions about possible symptoms you might someday develop and what they mean.

HOW MUCH DID YOU LEARN?

INSTRUCTIONS: Please <u>Circle</u> T for true, F for false, or the appropriate letter or write in your answer for each item. You may use the instructional materials you received if needed, but first try to answer each question unaided.

1. T F Epidemiological studies consistently find Obsessive Compulsive Disorder is relatively rare.

2. T F Even under optimal conditions, psychotropic medications provide most patients

    suffering from Obsessive Compulsive (OC) Disorders with than 40-60% relief.

3. T F The Prepontine Cistern is the region of the brain most frequently associated with OC disorders.

4. T F Obsessive Compulsive Personality Disorders (OCPD) is thought to be more biological in it's origins than Obsessive Compulsive Disorder.

5. T F O-OCD or "Pure Obsessions" are the most common form of obsessive-compulsive problem.

6. Developing "slogans" or affirmations is often helpful for the OC sufferer because:
    A. They provide a way to desensitize to the anxiety
    B. They act as reminders of skills one has developed in treatment.
    C. They reduce feelings of dissociation.
    D. They assist in keeping a steady pace in the recovery process.
    E. Both (b) and (d)
    F. (Both (a) and (d)

7. T F Trichotillomania is characterized by multiple motor tics and one or more vocal tics.

8. T F In *The OCD Cycle* "Obsession Inoculation" is the treatment strategy of choice for the "Compulsive" phase of the cycle.

9. The "One Second Rule" assists the OC patient in avoiding _____.

10. Children growing up with an OC disorder are likely to experience difficulties with:
    A. Sleep   B. Security and Safety
    C. Relationships   D. Congruency and Communication
    E. All of the above

11. Individuals with an OC disorder are more likely than normal to develop:
    A. Artistic abilities   B. Wanderlust
    C. Depression   D. Feelings of grandiosity

12. Name three tools for "Obsession Inoculation." _____ _____ _____

13. T F A dry mouth, tense muscles, racing thoughts, "tunnel vision" and gastrointestinal distress are all common symptoms of the "Moderate Stage" of anxiety.

14. T F "Self-medicators" provide the OC sufferer with only temporary relief from the struggles of dealing with their obsessions and compulsions.

15. Habit reversal training is typically *not* the primary treatment tool for:
    A. Trichotillomania   B. Body Dysmorphic Disorder
    C. Stereotypic Movement Disorders   D. Tourette's Disorder

16. T F In the "Second of the Five Stages of OC Recovery" much of the work of Exposure and Response Prevention behavior therapy has already been completed.

17. The best example of exposure-based therapy for Body Dysmorphic Disorder is:
    A. Removing mirrors from the patient's house.
    B. Advising the patient to avoid visiting plastic surgeons.
    C. Asking the individual to appear in public without special coverings for the area of their body they imagine is "defective".

18. T F The majority of the "16 Keys To Recovery" are devoted to lifestyle and self-care.

19. Which is *not* true of Serotonin Reuptake Inhibiting drugs:
    A. Initial worsening of symptoms may indicate an eventually favorable response.
    B Work better for primarily obsessional OCD than for primarily compulsive OCD.
    C. Cause sexual dysfunction in approximately 60% of patients.
    D. Often cause more side effects in complex and long-term patients.

20. T F All OC disorders have in common that they are driven or "fueled" by anxiety.

21. T F Support groups are typically *not* helpful for persons with OCD.

22. The *Seven Steps to Fighting OCD Episodes* are:

    _____   _____
    _____   _____
    _____   _____
    _____

23. T F Once an individual has developed a particular form of obsession (e.g. contamination, symmetry, scrupulosity) there is very little chance the individual will develop other forms or types of obsessions.

24. Exposure and Response Prevention can be categorized as which of the following forms of behavioral treatment:
    A. Progressive desensitization   B. Progressive escalation
    C. Habituation   D. Operant conditioning
    E. Both C and B   F. Both C and D

25. "Disqualifying the positive" is a common form of _____.

26. T F Exposure and Response Prevention behavior therapy is a form of desensitization.

27. The first main task in dealing with obsessions is to "separate oneself mentally from them". The Second main task is to _____.

28. T F The first step in treating an impulse control problem such as Trichotillomania is:
    A. Defining the process of thought distortion   B. Learning stimulus control strategies
    C. Massed negative practice   D. Assessment of the behavior

29. Which of the following is *not* a core fear of Hoarders:
    A. Financial difficulties   B. Missed opportunities
    C. Experiencing loss   D. Forgetting something important

30. An Integrative Healthcare option for alleviating depression associated with OC disorders that has compared favorably in research with SSRI prescription drugs and often works more rapidly is:
    A. Kava Kava   B. Passion Flower
    C. SAMe   D. Qigong

31. T F   Having an "Emergency Plan" on a "Carry Card" is an essential tool for relapse prevention.

32. T F   Epidemiological studies consistently find Obsessive Compulsive Disorder (OCD) is relatively rare.

33. T F   Under typical conditions, psychotropic medications provide 60% of OCD patients with approximately 30% relief.

34. Multi-Sensory Massed Exposure is useful with which of the following types of OCD?

    A. Global Obsessions
    B. O-OCD
    C. Scrupulosity
    D. Hypochondriasis
    E. All the above
    F. Both A and C

35. The "Five Principles" used to *develop Exposure and Response Prevention exercises* are:

_____   _____
_____   _____
_____

36. Which is *not* true of Serotonin Reuptake Inhibiting drugs and OCD:
    E.   Initial worsening of symptoms may indicate an eventually favorable response.
    F.   Work better for primarily obsessional OCD than for primarily compulsive OCD.
    G.   Cause sexual dysfunction in approximately 60% of patients.
    H.   Lead to a cure versus symptom reduction

37. Compulsive Hoarders are best treated in an office or laboratory setting
    TRUE   FALSE

38. Which of the following does NOT play a significant role in NM-OCSD:

    A. Blood-brain barrier
    B. Pro-inflammatory cytokines
    C. The corpus callosum
    D. Anti-neuronal antibodies

COMMENTS FROM PROFESSIONALS ABOUT THE CHALLENGES AND SOLUTIONS SEMINAR ON WHICH THIS MATERIAL IS BASED

(Names withheld for confidentiality.)

"Dr. Komor is extremely knowledgeable and expert in his specialty. The seminar is full of facts and new information on the intricacies of the brain and its involvement in OCD."
> - Miami, FL

""The presenter was very well prepared, professional, and knowledgeable about the subject. He added to his presentation by sitting examples, involving the audience and being on the cutting edge of research findings. Great Job! Should be a two day seminar!"
> - Miami, FL

"As a parent of a child with OCD the information was very through – highlighting all the options our doctors have not told us about up to now."
> - Phoenix, AZ

"Dr. Komor was great! He has a wonderful presentation style and did an excellent job."
> - Phoenix, AZ

"Wonderful ideas and lots of them."
> - Tucson, AZ

"This is information which has not been presented at any other workshop I have attended. It is very valuable and useful."
> - Tucson, AZ

"This was one of the most comprehensive and coherent presentations on the topic that I have has the pleasure of attending."
> - Tucson, AZ

"The best seminar I have attended. Excellent presentation (speaker, PowerPoint, etc.) and information."
> - Albuquerque, NM

"Fantastic presenter. Make it a two day seminar!"
> - Albuquerque, NM

"Nice to learn actual tools for therapist and client to use rather than all theory."
> - Pamela Allen, Albuquerque, NM

"Excellent and informative. Dr. Komor was succinct, amusing, and good with the audience."
> - Albuquerque, NM

"Dr Komor is an excellent speaker with a great sense of humor and good examples. Information was very valuable. Gave lot's of ideas on how to work with clients."
- Canton, OH

"Exceeded my expectations by far!"
- Columbus, OH

"Great workshop! Speaker very knowledgeable. This program needs to be two days!
- Columbus, OH

"Excellent seminar! From the prospective of 'a person with OCD' the Dr.'s sharing was appreciated and certainly recognizable. It's nice to hear the information from someone who has lived it."
- Columbus, OH

"Enjoyed Dr. Komor's presentation style and honesty. It was a bit odd when he said that he and Sponge Bob go places together. I thought he was kidding, but I wasn't sure!"
- Canton, OH

"The speaker was very knowledgeable and did an excellent job of holding our interest.
- Columbus, OH

"Dr. Komor is very real… It's obvious that he truly understands."
- Cleveland, OH

"Effective use of humor, excellent handout, and materials. Well organized."
- Canton, OH

"Speaker was excellent and informative. Great information on issues in practice!"
- Canton, OH

"Appreciated the excellent handbook. I felt the presenter's self-disclosure and humor where very helpful.
- Columbus, OH

"A lot of content, but was explained simple at a good rate to comprehend. Covered all learning objectives.
- Columbus, OH

"I really enjoyed the seminar and the information will help me in practice with my clients."
- Jacksonville, FL

"Best seminar I have seen on this subject. A lot of meat – very substantial!"
- Daytona Beach, FL

"Dr. Komor is obviously and expert in this area. Enjoyed his humor."
- Daytona Beach, FL

"Excellent presentation. A wealth of material and depth of knowledge."
- Orlando, FL

"Excellent delivery, knowledge-base, and overview. Could not be improved."
- Orlando, FL

"Speaker was captivating with a good sense of humor."
- Winston-Salem, NC

"An excellent learning experience. I was engaged from the beginning. Dr. Komor is very real and knowledgeable."
– Colorado

"Dr Komor is an excellent speaker with a great sense of humor and good examples. Information was very valuable. Gave lots of ideas on how to work with clients."
- Colorado

"Exceeded my expectations by far!"
- Ohio

"Great workshop! Speaker very knowledgeable. This program needs to be two days!
- Ohio

"Excellent seminar! From the prospective of 'a person with OCD' the Dr.'s sharing was appreciated and certainly recognizable. It's nice to hear the information from someone who has lived it."
- South Dakota

"Instructor is extremely knowledgeable!"
- South Dakota

"The speaker was very knowledgeable and did an excellent job of holding our interest.
- Arkansas

"Dr. Komor is very real… It's obvious that he truly understands."
- Louisiana

"Presenter was great!"
- Louisiana

"Effective use of humor, excellent handout, and materials. Well organized."
- Tennessee

"Speaker was excellent and informative. Great information on issues in practice!"
- Tennessee

"Appreciated the excellent handbook. I felt the presenter's self-disclosure and humor were very helpful.
- Florida

"Dr Komor is an excellent speaker with a great sense of humor and good examples. Information was very valuable. Gave lot's of ideas on how to work with clients."
- Ohio

"Excellent seminar! From the prospective of 'a person with OCD' the Dr.'s sharing was appreciated and certainly recognizable. It's nice to hear the information from someone who has lived it."
- District of Columbia

"Enjoyed Dr. Komor's presentation style and honesty. It was a bit odd when he said that he and Sponge Bob go places together. I thought he was kidding, but I wasn't sure!"
- Virginia

"Instructor is extremely knowledgeable!"
- Virginia

"The speaker was very knowledgeable and did an excellent job of holding our interest.
- Alabama

"Dr. Komor is very real… It's obvious that he truly understands."
- Colorado

"Presenter was great!"
- Ohio

"Effective use of humor, excellent handout, and materials. Well organized."
- Colorado

"Speaker was excellent and informative. Great information on issues in practice!"
- Wyoming

"Appreciated the excellent handbook. I felt the presenter's self-disclosure and humor where very helpful.
- Wyoming

"A lot of content, but was explained simple at a good rate to comprehend. Covered all learning objectives.
- Wyoming